Sonya Clark:
Monumental Cloth, The Flag We Should Know

Published by The Fabric Workshop and Museum and MW Editions

Contents

Foreword by Susan Lubowsky Talbott

5

We Hold These Truths by Valerie Cassel Oliver

11

"A Piece of Cloth That Brings a Nation to Its Knees" by W. Fitzhugh Brundage

21

Monumental and Many

29

Reconstruction Exercise

49

Lesson Plan (Confederate Truce Flag)

61

Reversals

71

Propaganda and Title Wall

85

About the Artist

92

Acknowledgments

93

About The Fabric Workshop and Museum

94

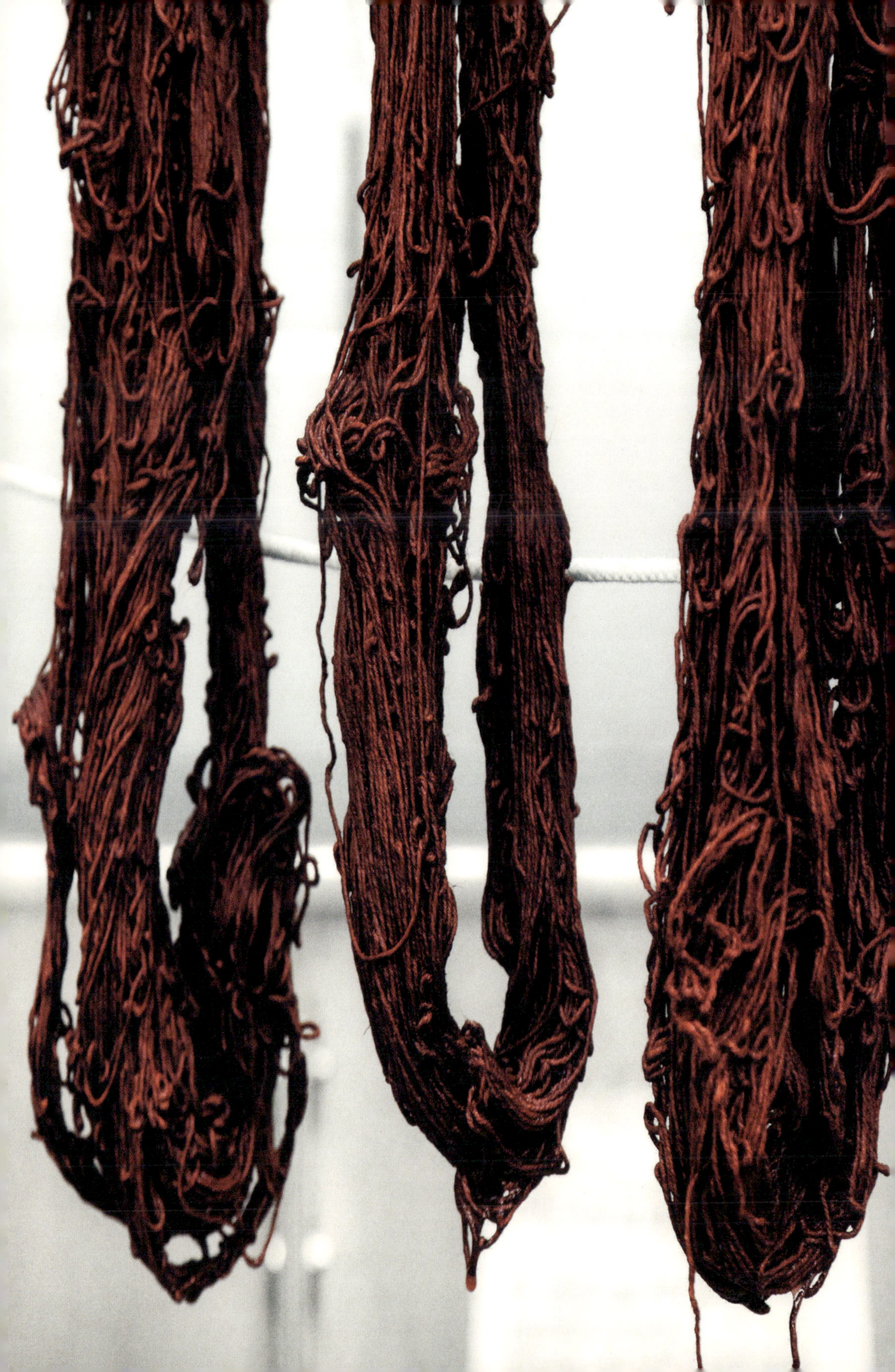

Foreword

When the Fabric Workshop and Museum (FWM) relocated to Arch Street in Philadelphia twelve years ago, it moved into the former National Flag and Banner Company building. So it is fitting that Sonya Clark's *Monumental Cloth, The Flag We Should Know* debuted in what was once a factory where flags were manufactured.

Clark's project begins with a significant but surprisingly little-known artifact: a humble white dishcloth that served as a makeshift flag of truce, initiating the end of the Civil War in 1865. She posits a huge idea: that this visually unassuming yet historically momentous flag replace the Confederate Battle Flag as a national emblem. At a time when our country is politically and culturally divided, Clark asks: "What if this were the symbol that endured?"

When a confederate soldier proffered that dishcloth to Union forces, it was transformed into the Confederate Truce Flag, which is now in the collection of the National Museum of American History, the Smithsonian Institution. For her work *Monumental*, Clark took the original dimensions of the dishcloth and enlarged them ten times, to fifteen-by-thirty feet. Together with *Many*, made of one hundred true-to-scale replicas of the original, this largely forgotten fragment of history is amplified both physically and symbolically. Clark makes it possible for the cloth that signalled peace to capture our collective imagination and correct a historical imbalance—and proposes that a symbol of reconciliation replace a symbol of division.

Two installations, *Reconstruction Exercise* and *Lesson Plan (Confederate Truce Flag)*, invite visitors to weave sections of the Truce Flag and make rubbings of its waffle-weave pattern. So by weaving and rubbing, visitors become actors in Clark's narrative.

In her emotionally charged performance *Reversals*, Clark wipes dust from the gallery floor to expose the text from the Preamble to the Declaration of Independence. Each element of this piece resonates with meaning, from her hand-sewn World War II-era dress (copied from the dress worn by Ella Watson in the 1942 Gordon Parks photograph *American Gothic, Washington, D.C.*) to the muddied dishcloth printed with an image of the Confederate Battle Flag, to her kneeling as she scrubs the floor, to the dust collected from nearby historic sites. As she reveals the famous lines from the Preamble to the Declaration of Independence, "We hold these truths to be self-evident, that all men are created equal," Clark pointedly draws a distinction between these idealistic words and our nation's lived history, referencing the Founding Fathers, the Civil War, the Great Depression, and finally Colin Kaepernick, the banished professional football player turned social justice activist.

The support of our funders was essential to the success of this landmark project. Major funding was provided by the Andy Warhol Foundation for the Visual Arts, Amherst College (for this catalogue), Agnes Gund, The National Endowment for

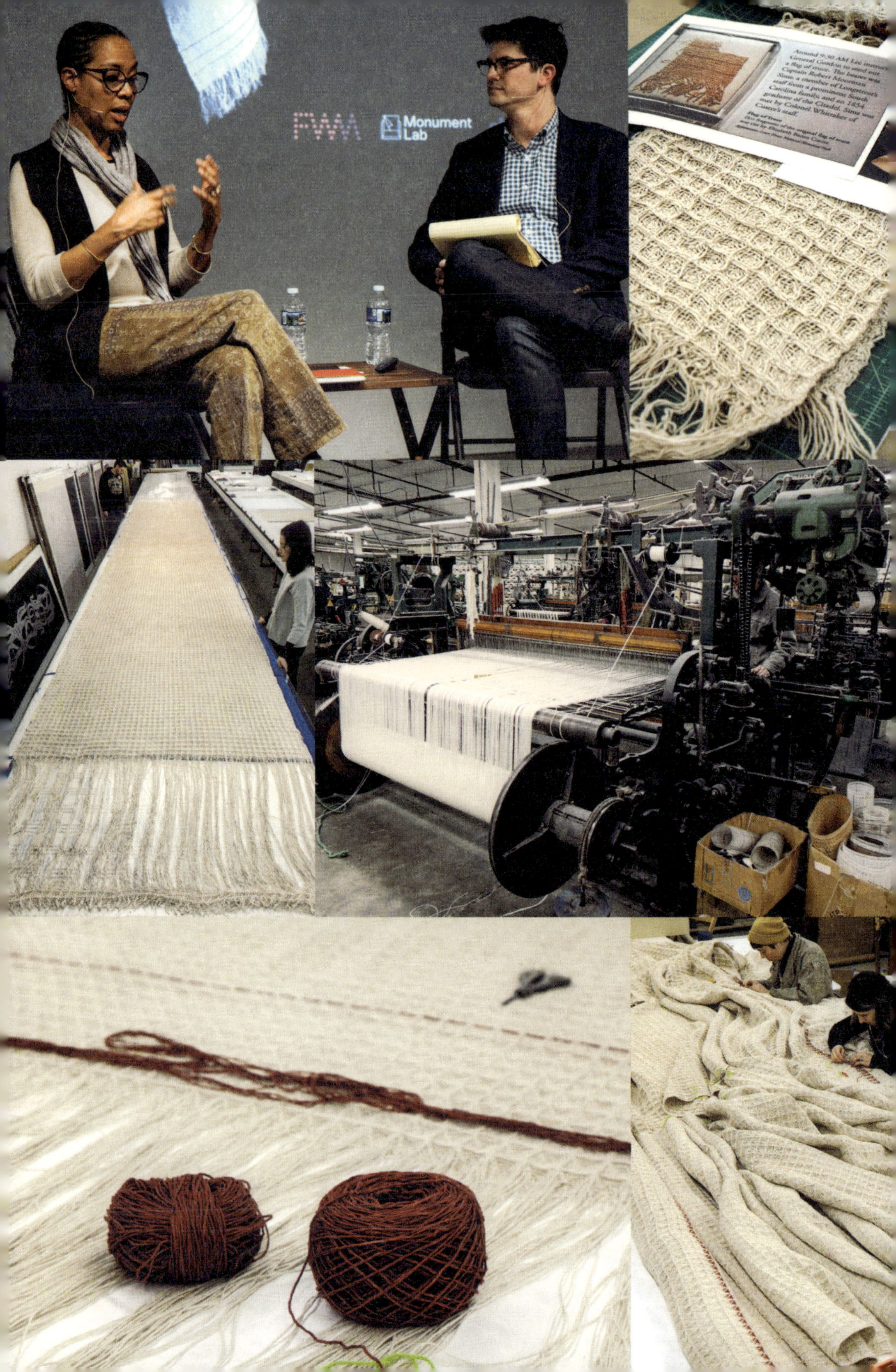

PWA
Monument Lab

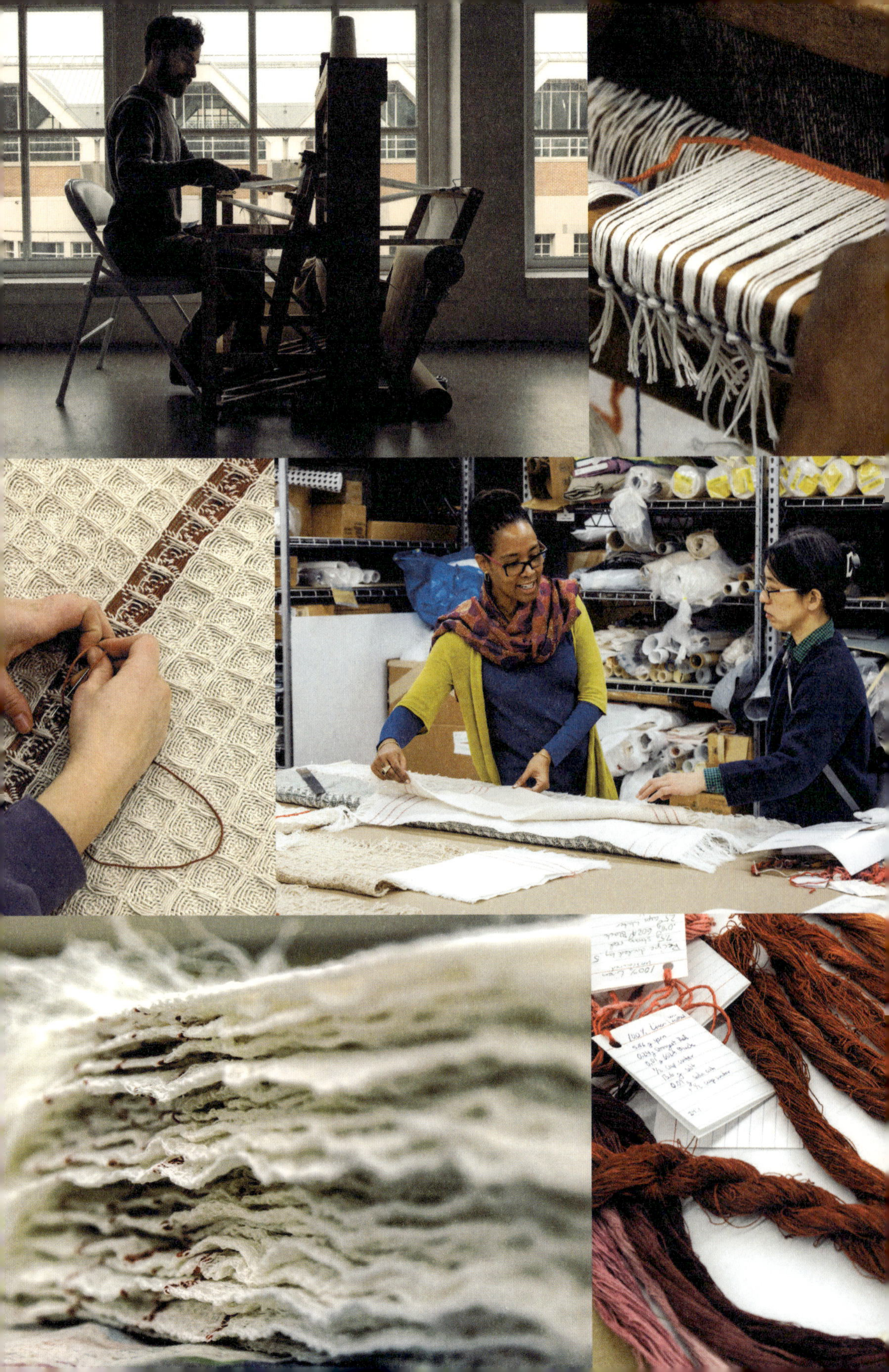

the Arts, Goya Contemporary Gallery, and Goya-Girl Press. I am also grateful to the individuals who provided additional support; they are listed in the acknowledgments at the end of this book, along with all those who contributed to realizing Clark's vision.

During her residency, Clark worked with the artists on FWM's studio staff to create each element of *Monumental Cloth*. Commercially woven, the enormous flag *Monumental* was sewn together and tea-stained at FWM. The flags in *Many* were hand-woven and made of historically accurate materials, including the madder dye used for the red stripes. Studio Director Nami Yamamoto oversaw production, with team members Avery Lawrence, Allen West (who wove sixty of the one hundred flags), Zack Ingram, Kelly Kuykendall, and Abby Lutz. Overall project coordination was supervised by Exhibitions Manager Alexander Unkovic. I am deeply grateful to them for their extraordinary efforts.

Many partnerships with Philadelphia organizations broadened our audience and added to the project. Director of Education Christina Roberts and her colleagues at FWM curated an impressive array of educational programs. I especially want to thank Dejay Duckett and her colleagues at the African American Museum in Philadelphia, which hosted Clark's concurrent exhibition *Self-Evident*. Together, we presented several important programs, including "Sounding the Ancestors" with Clark, Regina Carter, Jason Moran, and Guthrie Ramsey (who led the panel), and performances by Joyce Scott and the Onus trio. Other program highlights included Monument Lab's Live Podcast with Sonya Clark and Paul Farber, along with the scholarly talks "Truce, Resistance and the Legacy of Flags as Cultural Symbols," presented by Dr. W. Fitzhugh Brundage and "Raising the White Flag," a conversation between Dr. David Silkenat and Clark.

I am also appreciative of those who lent looms for the exhibition: Thomas Jefferson University, Philadelphia; Tyler School of Art, Temple University, Philadelphia; The University of the Arts, Philadelphia; and Becky Flax. Thanks also to the weavers who dressed the looms and instructed the public on their use.

Finally, I extend my gratitude to Dr. Brundage and Valerie Cassel Oliver for their scholarly contributions to this catalogue, and to Takaaki Matsumoto and his team for its elegant design.

Above all, I thank Sonya Clark for this timely and courageous investigation that asks, "What would it mean to the psychology of this nation if the Truce Flag replaced the flag associated with hate and white supremacy?"

Susan Lubowsky Talbott, *Executive Director,*
The Fabric Workshop and Museum

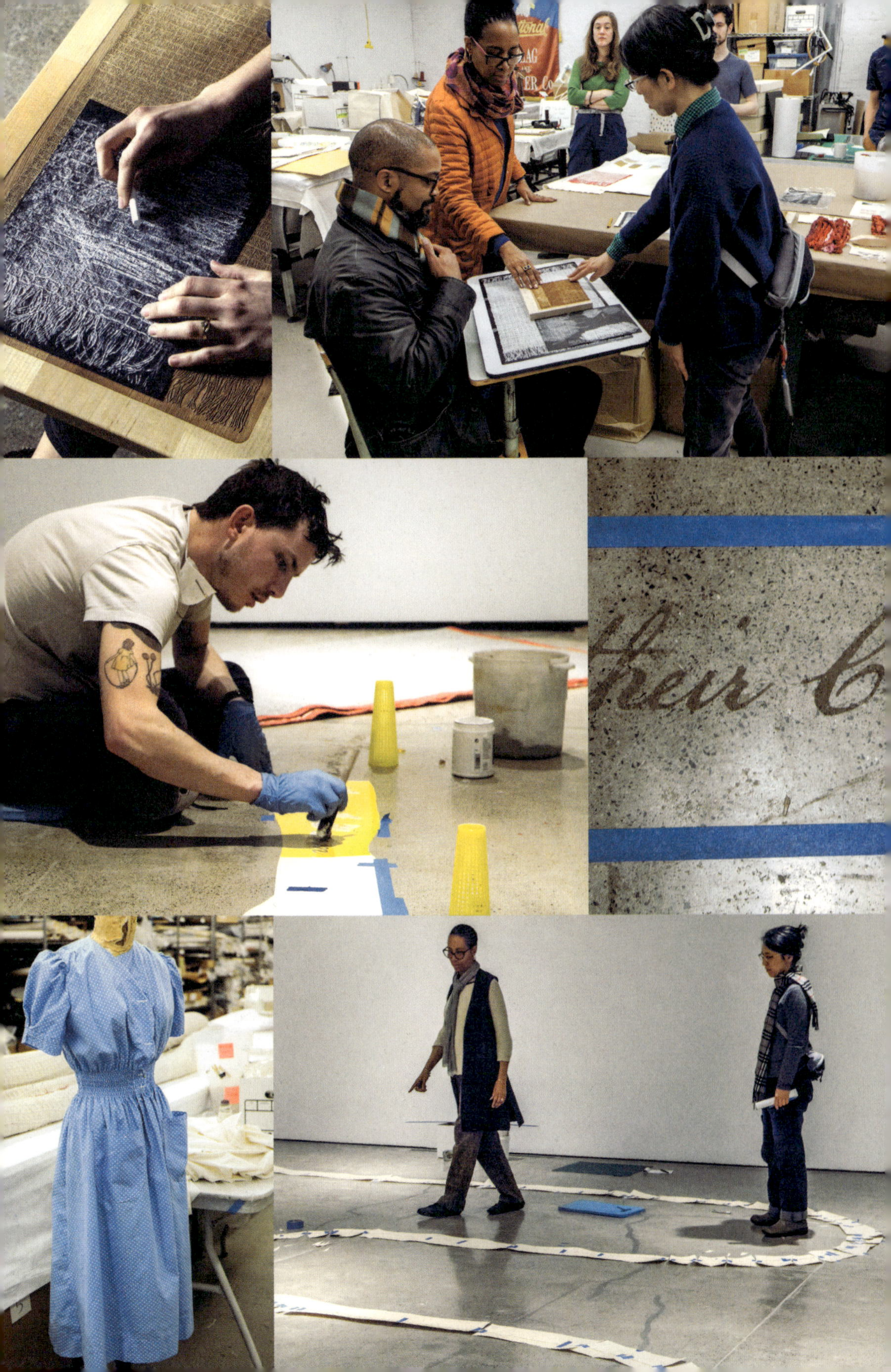

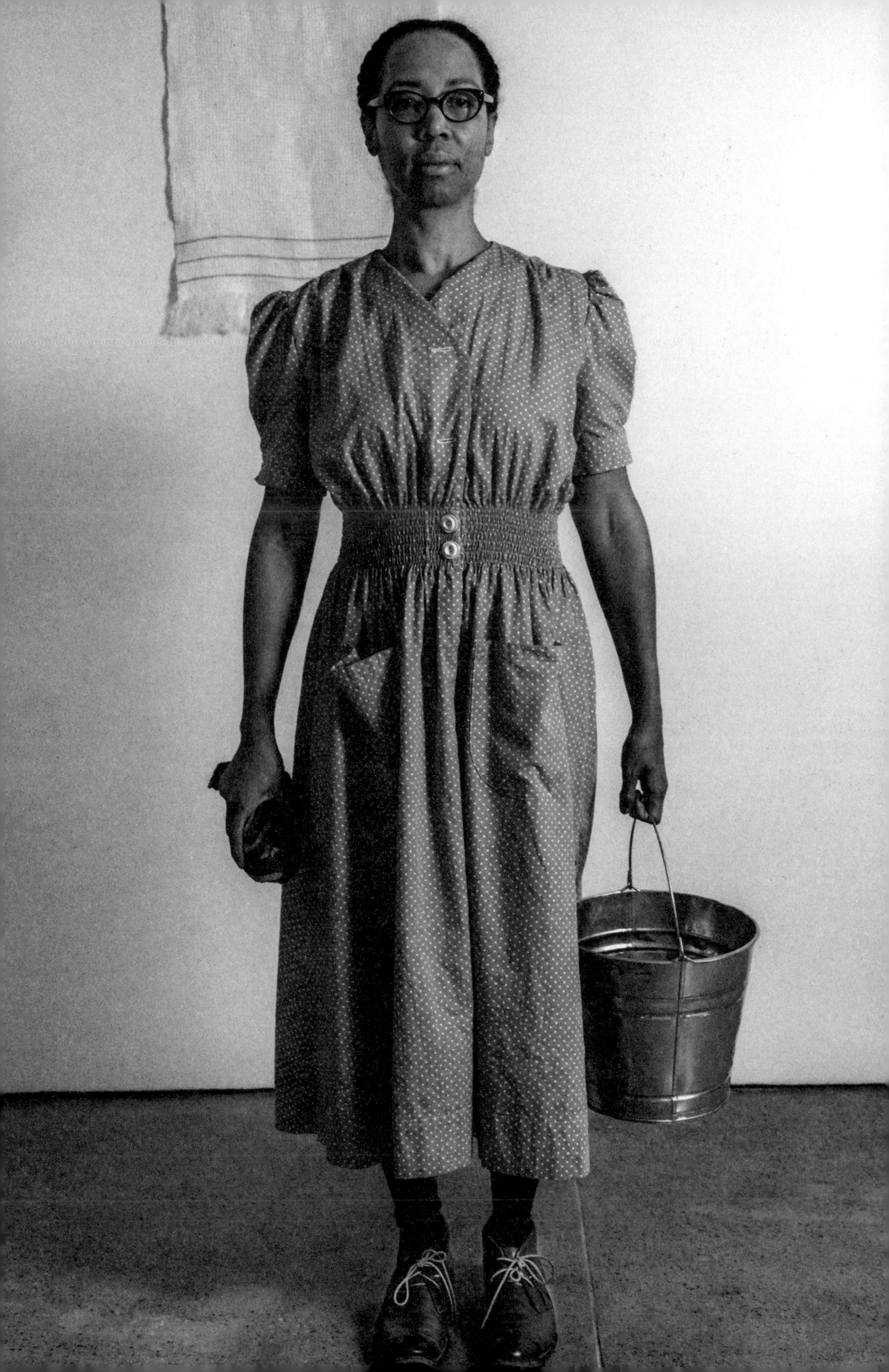

We Hold These Truths

by Valerie Cassel Oliver

Arbiters of history have often scrutinized the blurred lines and immense gulfs that divide fact from fiction. What is often mediated in the course of that scrutiny is the culture that seeks to uphold fiction in the face of fact. Such cultural insistence is born from a dogged determination to forge a foundational story that buttresses political and economic frameworks perpetuating a fictional narrative.

Such is the case with the propaganda that emerged in the wake of the Civil War. Anyone who has lived in the southern United States has at some point confronted the fiction of the Lost Cause. It asserts that the South's attempt at secession was a virtuous effort to maintain states' rights and repel aggression from the North. This false narrative never positions the predicament of millions of enslaved African Americans at the vortex of the events that led to the war, and it elides the white supremacist theories that supported their enslavement.

And so, what troubles the waters just beneath the surface in the Civil War chronicles of loss and reunification are the parallel narratives asserting that the South surrendered simply to get on with the business of rebuilding its cities and resuming its way of life. In the period of Reconstruction that followed the war, those who were once enslaved or relegated to the margins (such as freed Blacks) rose up from the fields and into the wooden seats of state and national congressional houses, as well as into seats of authority at hospitals, schools, universities, and private enterprises. For many sons and daughters of the Confederacy, Reconstruction has often been shunted to the footnotes of history or read as a simple inconvenience—an atonement for enslaving millions and then selfishly threatening to keep from

the North the lion's share of the economic wealth that their free labor built. This
is substantiated by the closure of the Freedmen's Bureau[2] in 1872 and the long
and arduous period that emerges in the wake of its absence. The reunified national
government—through the administrations of Presidents Andrew Johnson, Ulysses S.
Grant, and Rutherford B. Hayes—failed to uphold the progress that Reconstruction
promised or to squelch the establishment of the oppressive Jim Crow laws that codified
a racial apartheid system in the South. The inability of the federal government to
protect the rights of formerly enslaved people enabled white supremacist propaganda
to resurface and persist for more than a century. So entrenched is this propaganda
that even after the adoption of civil rights legislation in the mid-twentieth century,
the lie of white supremacy continues as the bedrock of resistance to issues ranging
from dismantling segregationist policies toward integration to current concerns about
equity and justice.

Perhaps the most enduring symbol of this fiction is what is commonly referred
to as the "rebel flag" or "battle flag" under which Confederate troops, led by General
Robert E. Lee of Richmond, Virginia, fought. During the war, Richmond was the
governmental seat of the Confederate States of America. The Confederate Battle Flag
has become an enduring signifier of a white supremacist ideology deeply rooted in the
zero-sum conception that Blacks are inherently inferior and that the economic power
of whites is dependent upon their subjugation. An existential imperative of white
supremacy is the maintenance of a social order enabling this economic structure.
So, it was not happenstance when, in 1948, the Confederate Battle Flag was embraced
as a symbol of the States' Rights Democratic Party, or the Dixiecrats, a short-lived
segregationist political faction. Within this context, the Battle Flag remains affixed
as a lasting symbol of a fictional heroic past deeply rooted in the wells of racism. And,
while there are some who celebrate this flag under the guise of a renewed interest in
the history of the South and ancestral links to the Confederacy, for millions of other
people it stands as an aching reminder of state-sanctioned racial and ethnic oppression.

Now in our contemporary social and political landscape—where overt racial
suppression is once again at the forefront of the national consciousness—we are
forced to scrutinize not only these persistent lies but also newly constructed fictions
that denigrate immigrants, women, and diverse ethnic and cultural communities and
undergird inequitable policies directed toward them. In the astute and prescient words
of James Baldwin, the "invented past," under the increasing weight of our current
political moment, is beginning to crumble. However, even as cities dismantle the
plaques, monuments, and street signs that have stood as symbols of Confederate
virtue, their black, brown, and immigrant citizens face a backlash of white supremacist
terror. It is a season of drought, and the fiction is disintegrating but not without the
desperate last gasps of life.

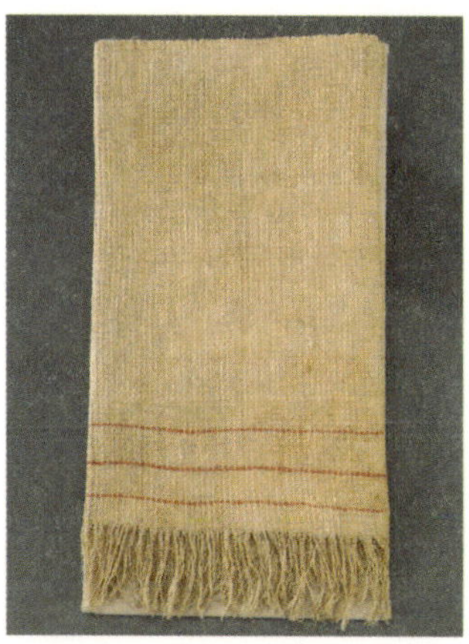

This dishcloth became the Confedrate Truce Flag on April 9, 1865, when General Robert E. Lee surrendered his Confederate army to Union General Ulysses S. Grant. Division of Political and Military History, National Museum of American History, Smithsonian Institution

A literary giant and political activist, Baldwin was among the many artists who lent their talents to fighting racial inequity during the civil rights era and after. The writer was relentless in exposing America's hypocrisy and injustice, specifically the myth of white superiority, whether asserted in intellectual discourse or on the rural back roads of the South. He was clear in framing the violence and hostility against African Americans within a legacy of a mythical history.

Sonya Clark emerges from this artistic lineage. Born in the District of Columbia and having spent more than a decade living in Richmond—with its avenue dedicated to the heroes of the Lost Cause—Clark has lent her sizable talents to dismantling the propaganda of Confederate iconography through both her fiber-based sculpture and her performance pieces. Her work *Unraveling* (2015–present, p. 16) is a literal deconstruction of the Confederate Battle Flag, collaborating with audience members to unravel the iconic segregationist symbol. And in a 2011 work titled *Black Hair Flag*, Clark reconfigured the Battle Flag, covering its surface with cotton threads that have been manipulated in African hairstyling techniques—cornrowed into stripes and Bantu-knotted into stars—to create an image of the U.S. flag on top of it. Clark frames a dialogue that brings the weighted corpus of Blackness to bear. Within the space of object and action, Clark insists that the contemporary moment serve as a corrective to the inaccuracies of the past. In performances where she engages an audience member with the Battle Flag, there is a suspension of time and, in the immediacy of action, shared intimacy. The stories whispered and confessions given over the shared dismemberment of this physical propaganda reframe the monolithic

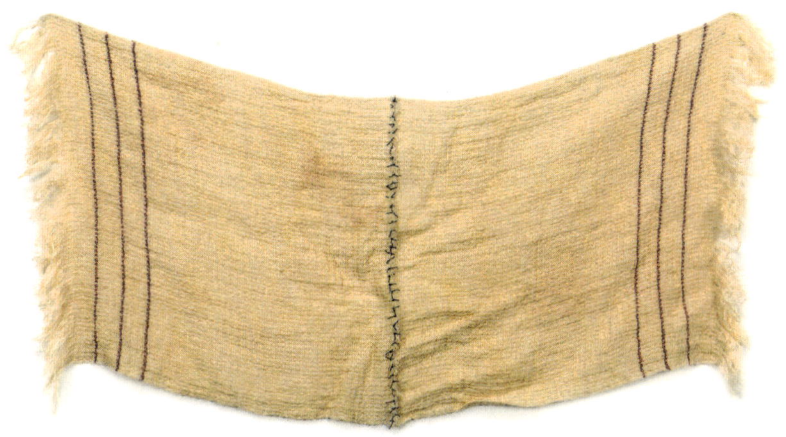

Sonya Clark. *Monumental Cloth (sutured)*, 2017. Tea-stained linen and silk suture thread, 20 x 34 inches (50.8 x 86.4 cm)

narrative of oppression—for both the oppressors and the oppressed. It is as Baldwin predicted: the fiction begins to crumble though the symbol remains.

Within this awareness, the artist moves beyond predictable symbolism and disavows attempts to balance fact with fiction. The flag we *should* know—the Truce Flag, which became the Confederate flag of surrender (p. 14)—offers the truth that at once disrupts and negates the myth and is what ought to be the enduring symbol. It is one half of a humble kitchen towel, now yellowed with age. On April 9, 1865, a captain in General Robert E. Lee's Army of Northern Virginia breached Union lines to offer that symbol of surrender to General Ulysses S. Grant at Appomattox Court House in Virginia. More than seventy years elapsed before Elizabeth Custer would give this historical relic to the nation in 1936. Between 1902 and 1919, the Commonwealth of Virginia, and in particular Richmond, erected monuments and memorials to its Confederate heroes—effectively reframing surrender as glorious defeat. In rewriting the narrative of the end of the Civil War, the South not only renounced its capitulation, but also constructed the social, political, and legislative armature of oppression that would continue the legacy of relegating Blacks to the economic and social margins.

It is here where Clark confronts the unvarnished realities of this legacy and asks, "What if this [the Confederate Truce Flag] was the symbol that endured rather than General Robert E. Lee's battle flag?" The question also points to the complicity of a unified nation in the collective oppression of Black bodies, as the apartheid system of Jim Crow was allowed to fester and spread, evolving to the white

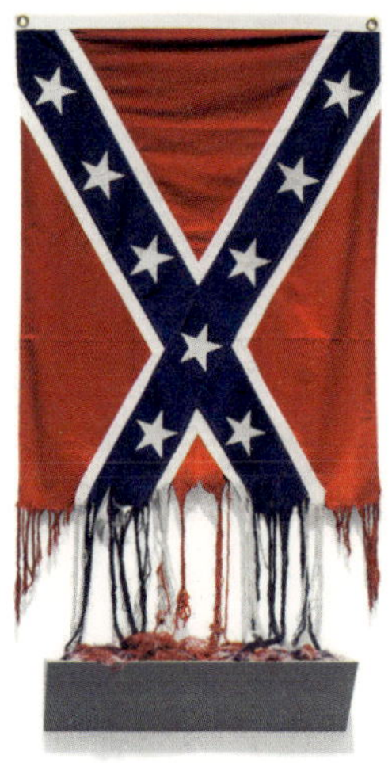

Sonya Clark. *Unraveling*, 2015–present. Cotton
Confederate battle flag. Dimensions variable.
Courtsey of the Pennsylvania Academy of Fine
Arts, Philadelphia. Museum Purchase

supremacist terrorism that exists today. For Clark, we must unlearn the propaganda
that has insidiously asserted itself into every aspect of life, as shown in the innumerable
commercial products proudly displaying the iconic symbol of hate—from baby onesies
to yoga mats and motor decals—some of which she lists in her work *Propaganda*
(2019, pp. 84, 86–89).

In the Fabric Workshop and Museum, Clark's *Monumental* (2019, pp. 28–35),
a fifteen-by-thirty-foot woven replica of the Confederate Truce Flag, and *Many* (2019,
pp. 31, 36–47), composed of one hundred actual-size replicas of the same flag, flank
a most telling monochromatic wall painting. *Title Wall* (2019, p. 91) is accompanied
by text at the bottom that simply notes, "Benjamin Moore Paint Color 2080-20:
Confederate Red," a color that the company only recently rebranded as "Patriotic
Red"—jaw-dropping though hidden in plain sight. Clark is pushing against the
normalization of propaganda, which can only be offset by putting forth histories
that drown out the fanfare of fiction.

Clark deliberately sets out to re-educate the public through a series of actions that
build a muscle memory of sorts. In her work *Lesson Plan* (2019, pp. 60–69), visitors
to the exhibition sit at school desks whose surfaces bear the raised markings of the
Truce Flag. They make rubbings with white chalk on black sheets of Tyvek, which
they can then take home. *Reconstruction Exercise* (2019, pp. 48–59) is a group of
small looms that visitors use with the aid of an assistant to weave a new Truce Flag.
The textile's "waffle" design, as the artist Joyce Scott has pointed out, evokes musical
stanzas that suggest the melancholy of atonement. For Clark, however, the activity

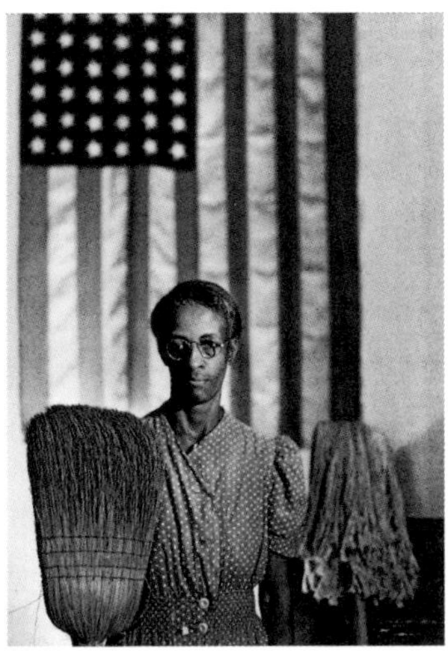

Gordon Parks (1912–2006) *American Gothic Washington, D.C.*, 1942. Courtesy of and © The Gordon Parks Foundation

gives the audience agency to collectively counter the propaganda of hate with acts that affix a new narrative.

The monumentality of Clark's work invites us to allow the story of the Truce Flag to inhabit our lives and to understand an almost erased history, which echoes and reverberates against the backdrop of a Benjamin Moore Confederate Red reality. That reality harbors the renewed scourge of terrorism enacted upon black and brown bodies, as well as upon women, in the name of white supremacist ideology; as in June 2015, when a white American man stepped into the historic Emmanuel African Methodist Episcopal Church in Charleston, South Carolina, during a mid-week bible study session and murdered nine Black people, hoping to provoke a race war. Now, as the forty-fifth president of the United States stokes intolerance and hate, this country is once again implicated in supporting a culture of terror, essentially doubling down on the violence enacted by its citizens. The terror is real, although its foundation is built upon lies. In the performance work *Reversals* (2019, pp. 70–83), Clark confronts complacency. In a plain cotton dress and work shoes similar to the clothing worn by Ella Watson, the subject of Gordon Parks's 1942 photograph *American Gothic, Washington, D.C.* (above), Clark displays the quiet temperament of resistance as she methodically washes a concrete floor covered in dust gathered from the Declaration House and Independence Hall in Philadelphia using a hand towel emblazoned with an image of the Confederate Battle Flag. As she wipes away the dust and wrings out the increasingly dirty towel, text from the Preamble to the Declaration of Independence is revealed:

We hold these truths to be self-evident, that all men are created equal, that they are endowed by their Creator with certain unalienable Rights, that among these are Life, Liberty and the pursuit of Happiness. That to secure these rights, Governments are instituted among Men, deriving their just powers from the consent of the governed, That whenever any Form of Government becomes destructive of these ends, it is the Right of the People to alter or to abolish it, and to institute new Government, laying its foundation on such principles and organizing its powers in such form, as to them shall seem most likely to effect their Safety and Happiness.

The language stands in stark opposition to the harsh reality not only of the late 1700s, when the document was written, but also in the subsequent centuries of government-sanctioned oppression that followed. Langston Hughes encapsulates this sentiment in the first few stanzas of his 1938 poem "Let America Be America Again":

> Let America be America again.
> Let it be the dream it used to be.
> Let it be the pioneer on the plain
> Seeking a home where he himself is free.
>
> (America never was America to me.)
>
> Let America be the dream the dreamers dreamed —
> Let it be that great strong land of love
> Where never kings connive nor tyrants scheme
> That any man be crushed by one above.
>
> (It never was America to me.)
>
> O, let my land be a land where Liberty
> Is crowned with no false patriotic wreath,
> But opportunity is real, and life is free,
> Equality is in the air we breathe.
>
> (There's never been equality for me,
> Nor freedom in this "homeland of the free.")[3]

In her most ambitious project to date, Clark forces us to confront a history that has remained invisible to most. The United States, and in particular the South, is beginning to come to terms with its invented past as its subjective and malleable narrative faces a day of reckoning. Americans can no longer afford to turn away as white terrorism invades elementary schools, shopping malls, and movie theaters. We are all implicated, just as we are all victims, as the lingering effects of white supremacist propaganda infiltrate the thinking of even the "most woke" among us. Injustice is a pernicious cancer upon the foundational ideal of equality. Clark offers up the alternative: truth as both a shelter in this time of storm and a balm for the future. We must hold this truth as self-evident—that the historicized myth will crumble in the heat of a new day.

1. James Baldwin, "The Fire Next Time," in *Collected Essays*, ed. Toni Morrison (New York: Library of America, 1998), 121.

2. The Freedmen's Bureau was established in 1865 by President Abraham Lincoln, during the waning days of the Civil War. Its primary purpose was to assist formerly enslaved people, along with other displaced people, in the aftermath of the war.

3. Langston Hughes, "Let America Be America Again," in *The Collected Poems of Langston Hughes*, ed. Arnold Rampersad (New York: Vintage Classics, 1995), 189–90.

Valerie Cassel Oliver is the Sydney and Frances Lewis Family Curator of Modern and Contemporary Art at the Virginia Museum of Fine Arts in Richmond. Ms. Cassel often focuses on representation, inclusivity, and highlighting artists of different social and cultural backgrounds. In 2000, she was a co-curator of the Whitney Biennial at the Whitney Museum of American Art, New York.

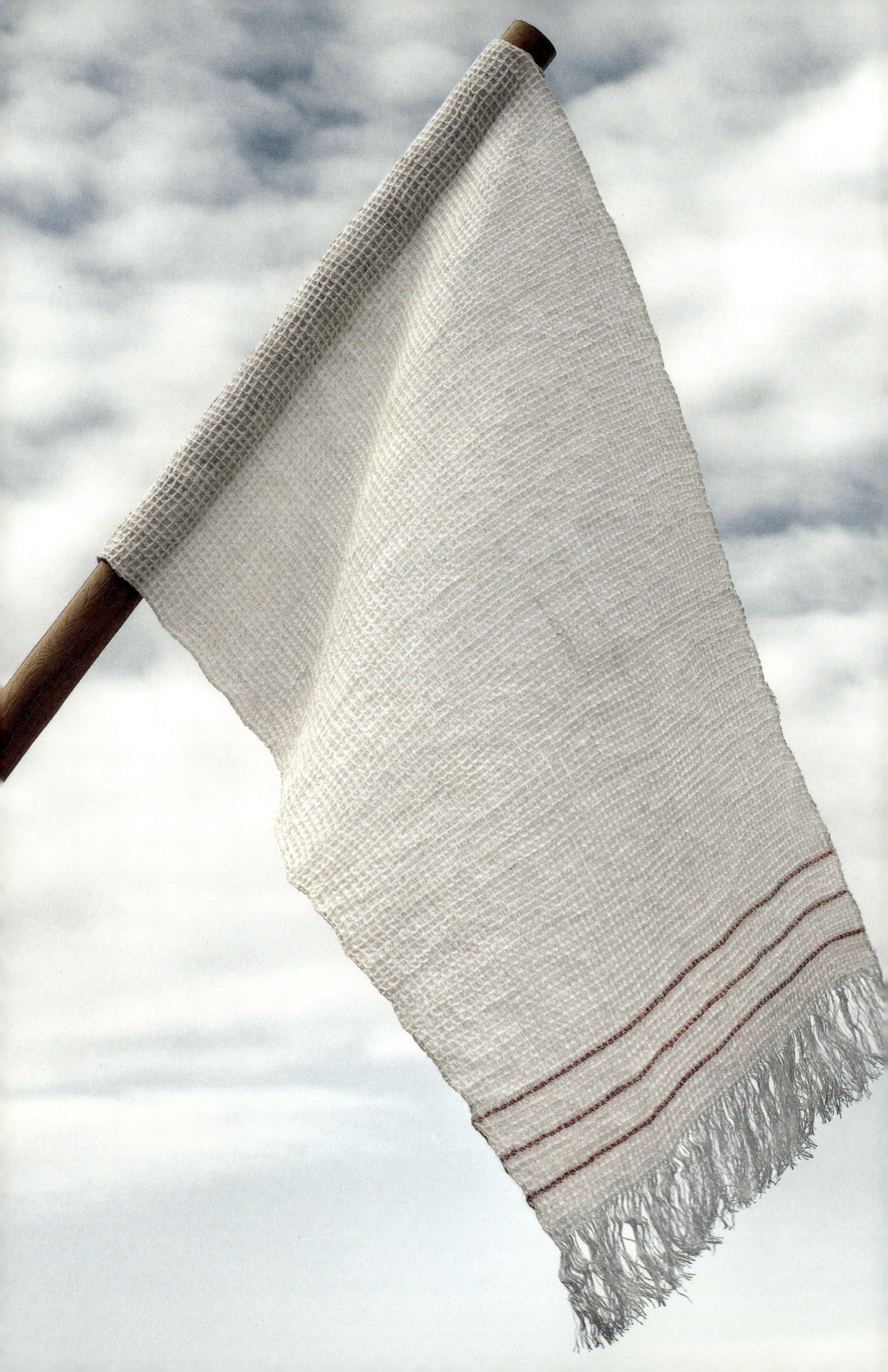

"A Piece of Cloth That Brings a Nation to Its Knees"

W. Fitzhugh Brundage

A flag, Afro-Guyanese playwright and poet John Agard observes, is "a piece of cloth/That makes the guts of men grow bold."[1] Light enough to flap languidly in the breeze, a flag may yet bear the symbolic weight of a society's loftiest ideals or bitterest grievances. The flags that Americans displayed during the nation's Civil War were no exception.

It seems inconceivable that Americans could have waged the Civil War without flags. Flags, as Agard emphasizes, stoke martial fervor—no military muster is complete without unfurled standards. Millennia before the Confederate army fired the opening shots of the Civil War at Fort Sumter in April 1861, ancient Romans understood the value of military banners, and medieval-era armies throughout Europe boasted colorful military ensigns. In early modern times, especially when weaponry became lethal at greater distances, flags became essential to distinguish friend from foe on the battlefield. For battle-hardened soldiers, flags were revered symbols of unit pride. Losing one to the enemy was especially ignominious. After the Civil War, the fate of captured Confederate flags sparked bitter quarrels between those Union veterans who advocated returning them to Confederate veterans as a gesture of reconciliation and others who recoiled at extending any honor to would-be destroyers of the republic.

As these symbolic pieces of fabric should, the standards of the Union and the Confederacy expressed how each side viewed itself and wanted to be viewed by others. The Union flag pointedly ignored the secession of the southern states. It was identical in design to the prewar flag, displaying thirty-four stars, one for each state in the union in 1861, including all of the states that participated in the southern rebellion. (In 1863, a thirty-fifth star was added when West Virginia joined the Union.) Its virtually unchanged design was consonant with President Abraham Lincoln's belief that the southern rebellion was a tragic but ephemeral threat to "the mystic chords of memory" that bound the American people to the union.[2] Because the flag that Union troops marched beneath was consistent with the national flag before and after the conflict, it never became associated exclusively with the war in the American imagination. After the war some embittered white southerners did regard it as a symbol of Yankee tyranny, but their resentment mellowed, and by the end of the nineteenth century the American flag was the uncontested symbol of national pride.

The Confederacy was at war throughout its brief life and, consequently, its flags were those of war. Befitting a newly birthed and inchoate nation, the Confederacy had several official flags. The first, which was dubbed the "Stars and Bars," closely resembled the Union flag, underscoring the insurgents' claims of being the true defenders of the republic's traditions—as opposed to the Yankees, who purportedly subverted them. But because the first Confederate flag was easily mistaken for the Union flag on the battlefield, Confederate armies, especially the Army of Northern

Virginia led by General Robert E. Lee, adopted a different design, the so-called Confederate Battle Flag. That a battle flag became the single most identifiable symbol of the Confederacy is apt. The survival of the Confederacy was inseparable from the success of its armies. The southern republic was only two months old when Confederate batteries opened fire on Fort Sumter, and it collapsed as soon as its armies could no longer withstand the Union onslaught.

Eight decades later, white southerners reaffirmed the association of the Confederate Battle Flag with resistance and belligerence when they unfurled it during their protracted campaign to thwart racial equality and preserve segregation. In 1948, the States' Rights Democratic Party (also known as the Dixiecrats) adopted the Battle Flag as a party emblem when it bucked the Democratic Party and contested the selection of Harry S. Truman, the incumbent president, as the nominee for the 1948 presidential election. The Dixiecrats formulated a pro-segregation platform and supported the candidacy of Governor Strom Thurmond of South Carolina. Subsequently, genteel white supremacists who opposed school integration wrapped themselves in the flag after the Supreme Court ruled in *Brown v. Board of Education* (1954) that segregated schools were unconstitutional. So too did the revived Ku Klux Klan and other white supremacist terrorists of the 1950s. By the early 1960s, the display of a Confederate Battle Flag decal on an automobile bumper or in the front yard of a private home was an unambiguous and potent endorsement of southern white nationalism.

The defeat of southern white resistance to desegregation and legal equality for African Americans during the 1960s had contradictory consequences for the proliferating uses and meanings of the Confederate Battle Flag. With each passing year, the flag appeared on an increasing number of consumer items, most of which would have offended the sensibilities (and taste) of the founders of the United Daughters of the Confederacy (UDC) and other Confederate heritage groups. From its founding in 1894 until the mid-twentieth century, the UDC had denounced the commercial exploitation of Confederate symbols and had scolded anyone who made inappropriate use of the flags of the southern republic. By the 1960s, however, the UDC and allied groups no longer retained sufficient prestige or influence to prevent unfettered merchandizing of the Confederate Battle Flag. As a result, it became so ubiquitous that some white southerners (and non-southerners) presumed that it now was merely a benign consumer talisman of white southern identity—Sonya Clark's *Propaganda* (2019, pp. 84, 86–89) lists dozens of commercial products that use it as a graphic symbol. But no matter how many Confederate Battle Flag bikinis, bandanas, beer can holders, and other gewgaws were produced and purchased, for many Americans, especially African Americans, the flag retained its close associations with the defense of slavery and white supremacy.

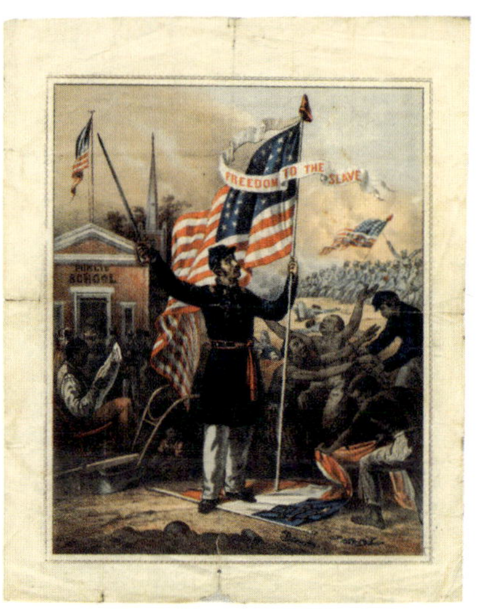

Union Recruitment handbill for African American soldiers,
c. 1863. Division of Political and Military History, National
Museum of American History, Smithsonian Institution

As the "solid" South gave way to the desegregated Sunbelt South, and migrants from elsewhere in the United States, Latin America, and Asia settled across the southern states, the persistent popularity of the Battle Flag underscored the challenges to meaningful pluralism in a region with no tradition of tolerating diversity. The region had always had a diverse population, but never had its institutions been open to all of its residents. During the 1970s, for the first time in the South's history, white southerners had to share both power and the public sphere with all of their fellow southerners.

This advent of civic pluralism during the last decades of the twentieth century necessarily provoked discussions about the persistence of Confederate symbols— especially the Battle Flag—that were emblems of white resistance to pluralism. After a white supremacist committed a mass shooting of nine African Americans in June 2015 during a bible study session at Emanuel African Methodist Episcopal Church in Charleston, South Carolina, tolerance for displays of the Battle Flag in civic spaces in the South waned. But even as elected officials removed the flag from public spaces, defenders of Confederate heritage countered by raising massive Battle Flags on private property alongside major thoroughfares. Nonetheless, the quarantine of the Confederate Battle Flag from public spaces has continued to the present moment, and is now virtually complete. Some white southerners still proclaim that the Battle Flag is a symbol of "heritage, not hate," but white nationalists, who give it pride of place beside Nazi and other contentious symbols in public rallies and on social media, have cemented its association with contemporary bigotry and violence.

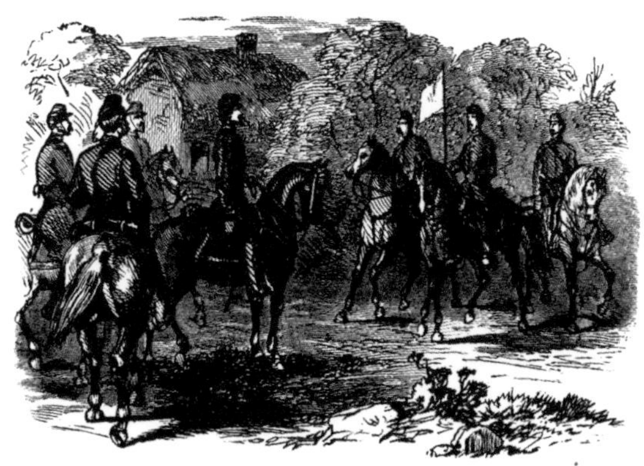

"Flag of Truce from the Confederates for a suspension of firing, to bury their dead, at Port Royal, S. C.," in Frank Leslie, *Frank Leslie's Illustrated Famous Leaders and Battle Scenes of the Civil War* (New York: Mrs. Frank Leslie, 1896), p. 482

Flags, Sonya Clark reminds us, can be emblems of concord as well as strife. They can convey humility as well as bravado. They can be precursors of peace as well as catalysts for war. They can signal a cautious appeal for an interruption in bloodletting. The artifact that has inspired the work that Clark created for this exhibition, an ordinary woven dishcloth, was transformed into a truce flag when Capt. R. M. Sims, a Confederate officer, used it to secure protection while traversing Union lines in April 1865 to request the suspension of hostilities and the commencement of negotiations for the surrender of General Lee's Army of Northern Virginia.

It was fitting that a commonplace piece of fabric served as the truce flag for the Civil War. As momentous as the surrender at Appomattox was for the nation, surrender itself was a commonplace experience during the war. The honorable surrender of a combatant to a foe was a testament to ideals of civilized warfare shared by northerners and southerners alike. Americans assumed that only fanatics fought to the death rather than surrender and that only barbarians put their vanquished foes to death. One out of every four Civil War soldiers surrendered at some point. As historian David Silkenat explains, the number of soldiers who surrendered is approximately equal to the number of soldiers killed. Roughly 450,000 Confederates and 200,000 Union soldiers surrendered in the war. Formal surrenders of large numbers of men, such as after the capture of Vicksburg in 1863, account for roughly half of these totals. The remainder took place before, during, or after battles when individual soldiers surrendered.[3]

This quotidian experience of surrender has no place in the American national memory though. The Civil War is recalled, especially in American popular culture, for heroic infantry charges and conspicuous acts of personal courage. The often complex circumstances, motivations, and consequences of surrender cannot easily be squared with our romantic images of the war. Some combatants surrendered at the first convenient opportunity so as to escape the carnage. Some surrendered when caught off-guard or in embarrassing circumstances. Others did so to avoid threatened annihilation by the enemy. Many of these men were "paroled" and pledged not to take up arms for a specified period. But for more than 100,000 soldiers, surrender led to extended captivity in prison camps, where alarming numbers of men succumbed to dysentery, diarrhea, pneumonia, and other diseases. For the several hundred thousand African Americans who fought for the Union, surrender was especially fraught. Regardless of whether Black prisoners had been free or enslaved before the war, Confederate authorities often re-enslaved them and returned them to their previous owners, or sold them off to new owners, or impressed them to work for the Confederate military. Thus, while surrender enabled some to survive the war unharmed, it condemned many others to an agonizing death in prison camps or to the thralldom of enslavement.

Sonya Clark understands that a flag of truce is an ambiguous symbol. It precedes negotiations that may have unexpected outcomes. The sincerity of the negotiations is likely to be contingent upon the relative strength and fatigue of the combatants. If one side is exhausted, a possible outcome is capitulation, in which case a truce flag may halt grievous suffering and senseless loss of life. The Confederate surrender at Vicksburg in 1863, for example, ended the misery of tens of thousands of starving civilians and soldiers. But when both warring sides retain resolve, another possible outcome is a resumption of combat. When Confederate General Nathan Bedford Forrest sent a flag of truce to Col. Stephen G. Hicks, the besieged Union commander of Fort Pillow, Tennessee, in April 1864, Hicks rebuffed it. Forrest had demanded the Union garrison surrender, warning, "Should my demand be refused, I cannot be responsible for the fate of your command."[4] When Hicks rejected his terms, Forrest ordered the capture of the fort. In the ensuing combat, Confederates killed or mortally wounded nearly three hundred Union soldiers (roughly half of the garrison). They singled out African-American soldiers for execution even while sparing white Unionists. In this instance, a flag of truce heralded a massacre.

The negotiations at Appomattox in April 1865 presaged an altogether less decisive outcome. General Lee's surrender to General Ulysses S. Grant marked the beginning of the end of the military phase of the Civil War. But almost every other major issue associated with the outbreak and consequences of the war remained unresolved. While the Confederate army laid down arms at Appomattox and elsewhere, the challenge of securing the loyalty of former Confederates remained. As Lincoln mulled in his last speech on April 11, 1865, the task was now to "mould from, disorganized and discordant elements" a restored nation.[5] On what terms would the nation be reunited? Would, as white southerners hoped, the prewar order be restored? Or did peace signal a second revolution, during which the nation would be reestablished on a new foundation? How had the conflict changed the nature and content of citizenship? What now was the status of African Americans? Did the Supreme Court's decision of *Dred Scott v. Sanford* in 1857 still hold, so that African Americans had no constitutional rights that whites were obliged to acknowledge? Did Confederates who had fought to destroy the Union retain their rights as citizens? What form of labor would replace slavery? Did the nation have any obligation to compensate formerly enslaved African Americans for their labor and suffering? While all of these questions were under discussion before Capt. Sims fashioned his flag of truce from a dishcloth, they took on new urgency as soon as the opposed armies gathered around Appomattox Court House to negotiate terms of surrender.

Sonya Clark asks us to imagine the Confederate Truce Flag as our national reminder of the cataclysm and bloodletting that laid the foundation for the nation we live in today. Our national flag is burdened with the entire history of this republic; its symbolic meaning cannot easily be reduced to an emblem of the Civil War and of emancipation. While the Confederate Battle Flag has rallied southern whites at various times during the past century and a half, it has never expressed the aspirations of more than a fraction of southerners, let alone Americans. It will forever be a symbol of the militant resistance to the abolition of slavery during an age of emancipation. Is there any more appropriate symbol of the war for us today than the Truce Flag, which reminds us of the Civil War's costs, its ambiguous resolution, and its unfulfilled promise?

1. John Agard, "Flag," in *Half-Caste and Other Poems* (London: Hodder Children's Books, 2004), 24. The title of this essay is also taken from Agard's poem.
2. Abraham Lincoln, First Inaugural Address (March 4, 1861), in Abraham Lincoln, *The Gettysburg Address* (London: Penguin Books, 2009), 113–14.
3. David Silkenat, *Raising the White Flag: How Surrender Defined the American Civil War* (Chapel Hill: University of North Carolina Press, 2019).
4. Scott, Robert N., Henry Martyn Lazelle, et.al. *The War of the Rebellion: a compilation of the official records of the Union and Confederate armies* (Washington, D.C.: Government Printing Office, 1880–1901), Series I, vol. 32, 547.
5. Abraham Lincoln, Final Public Address (April 11, 1865), in Abraham Lincoln, *The Gettysburg Address* (London: Penguin Books, 2009), 124–25.

W. Fitzhugh Brundage is the William Umstead Distinguished Professor of History at the University of North Carolina at Chapel Hill. He focuses on U.S. history since the Civil War. Dr. Brundage is the author of many books, including *Civilizing Torture: An American Tradition* (Belknap Press, 2018), which was nominated for the Pulitzer Prize in History.

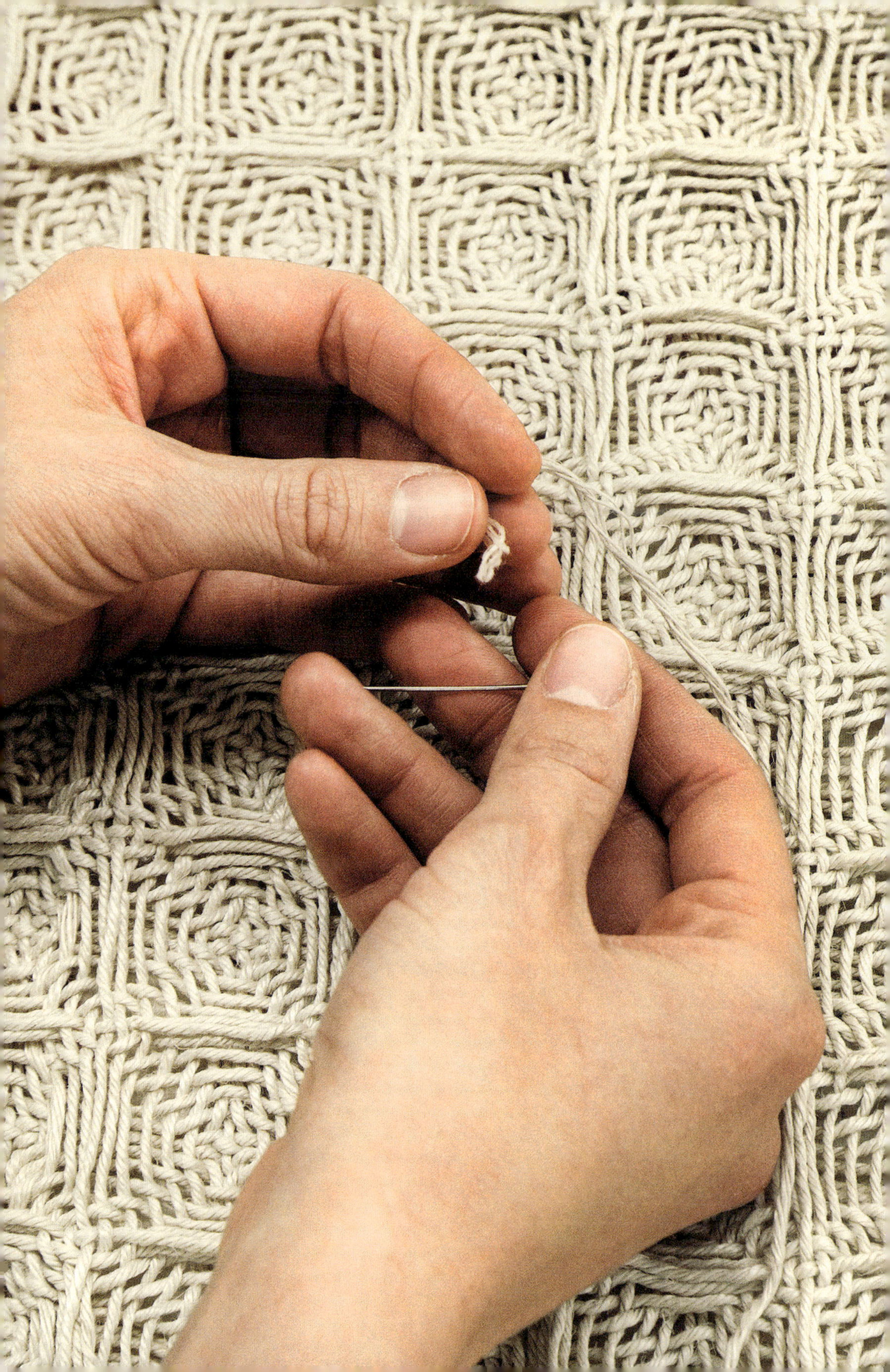

Monumental

On April 9, 1865, a humble textile became a historical artifact. Near Appomattox Court House in Virginia, General Robert E. Lee and his Confederate troops surrendered to General Ulysses S. Grant and the Union Army by presenting them with a common dishcloth. The white cloth with thin red stripes, now known as the Confederate Truce Flag, marked the end of the Civil War, a war that divided a nation, spanned four years, and claimed over 600,000 lives. Although the largest remaining portion of the Truce Flag is in the collection of the National Museum of American History in Washington, D.C., this emblem of the Civil War's final moments has been largely forgotten until now.

Monumental amplifies the scale and presentation of the Truce Flag. The massive re-creation had to be woven in three parts on an industrial loom and then stitched together by hand. The fifteen-by-thirty-foot piece measures ten times the size of the original flag, in a display reminiscent of another cloth housed at the National Museum of American History, the Star Spangled Banner. *Monumental* is tea-stained to match the artifact, now yellowed with age. The yarn used to weave the red stripes was dyed with madder root, as were the stripes in the original. And the replication of the complex waffle-weave structure indicates the primary purpose of the dishcloth that became the Truce Flag—to absorb.

Many

Many consists of one hundred true-to-size replicas of the Truce Flag woven with traditional methods and historically accurate dyes and patterns. Each one of the flags is bright white, emphasizing that they are newly created. In this way, *Many* mimics the strategy of production, repetition, and representation of other historical symbols as a way to perpetuate it in the imagination.

An adjacent corner in the space presents a wall displaying the question: "What if this were the symbol that had endured?" Next to this is a gathering space for contemplation, education, and conversation containing tables filled with books that address issues of American history, social justice, and civil rights.

Left, pages, 30–35: *Monumental,* 2019. Woven linen, madder dye, and tea stain. 180 x 360 inches (457.2 x 914.4 cm). In collaboration with The Fabric Workshop and Museum, Philadelphia
Pages 31, 40–47: *Many,* 2019. One hundred hand-woven linen cloths and madder dye. 18 ½ x 36 inches (47 x 91.4 cm) each. In collaboration with The Fabric Workshop and Museum, Philadelphia

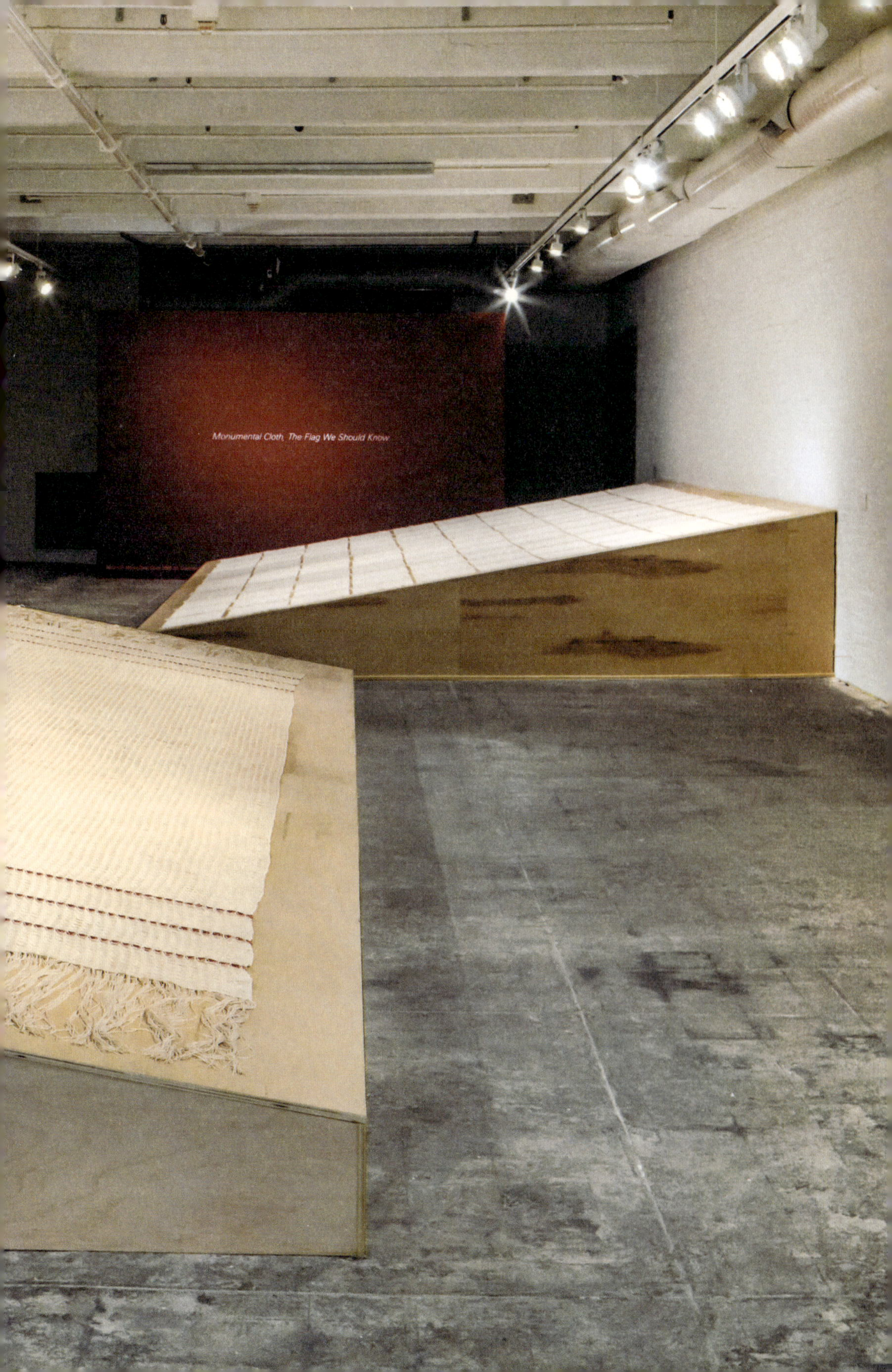

Monumental Cloth, The Flag We Should Know

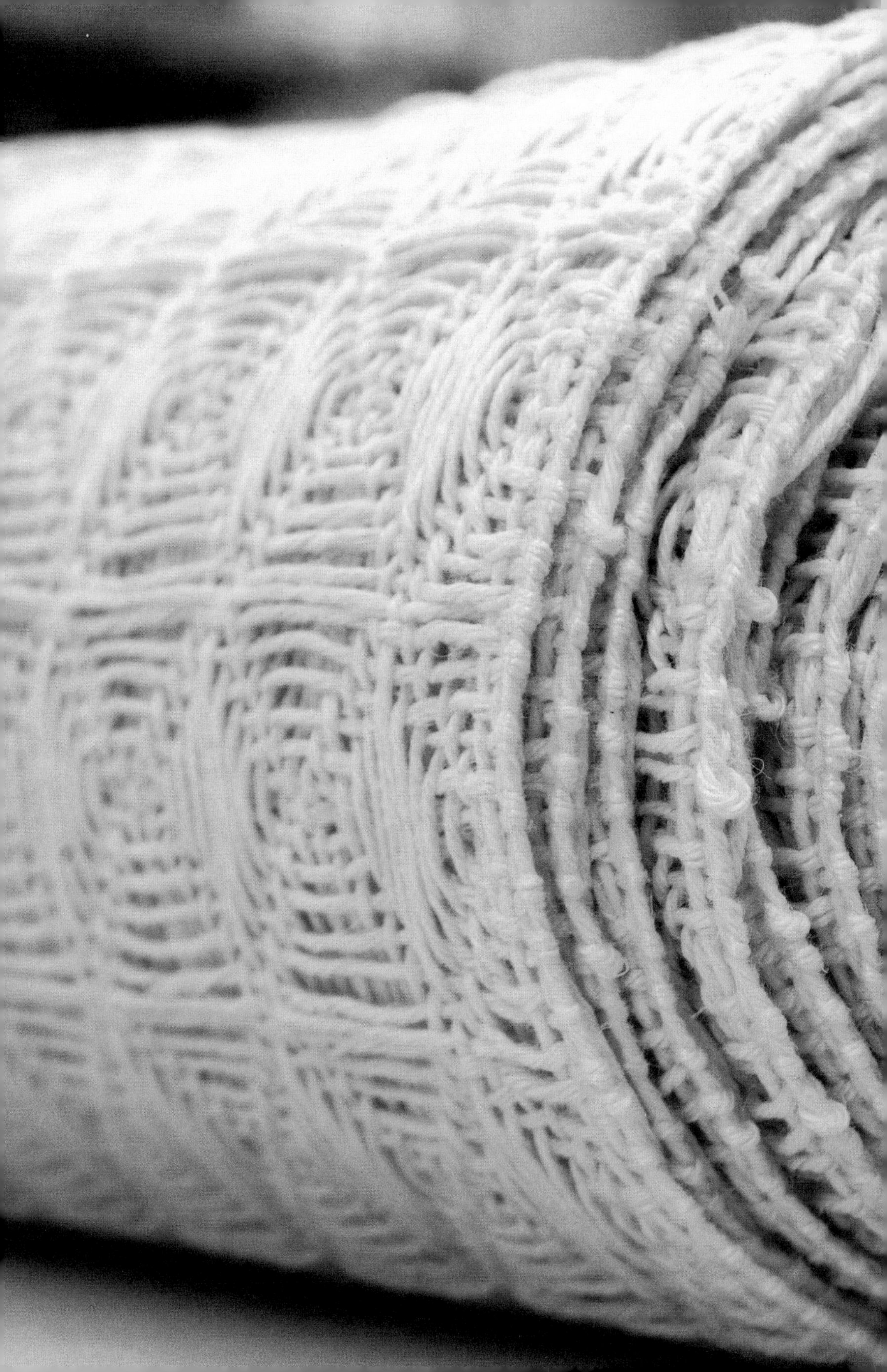

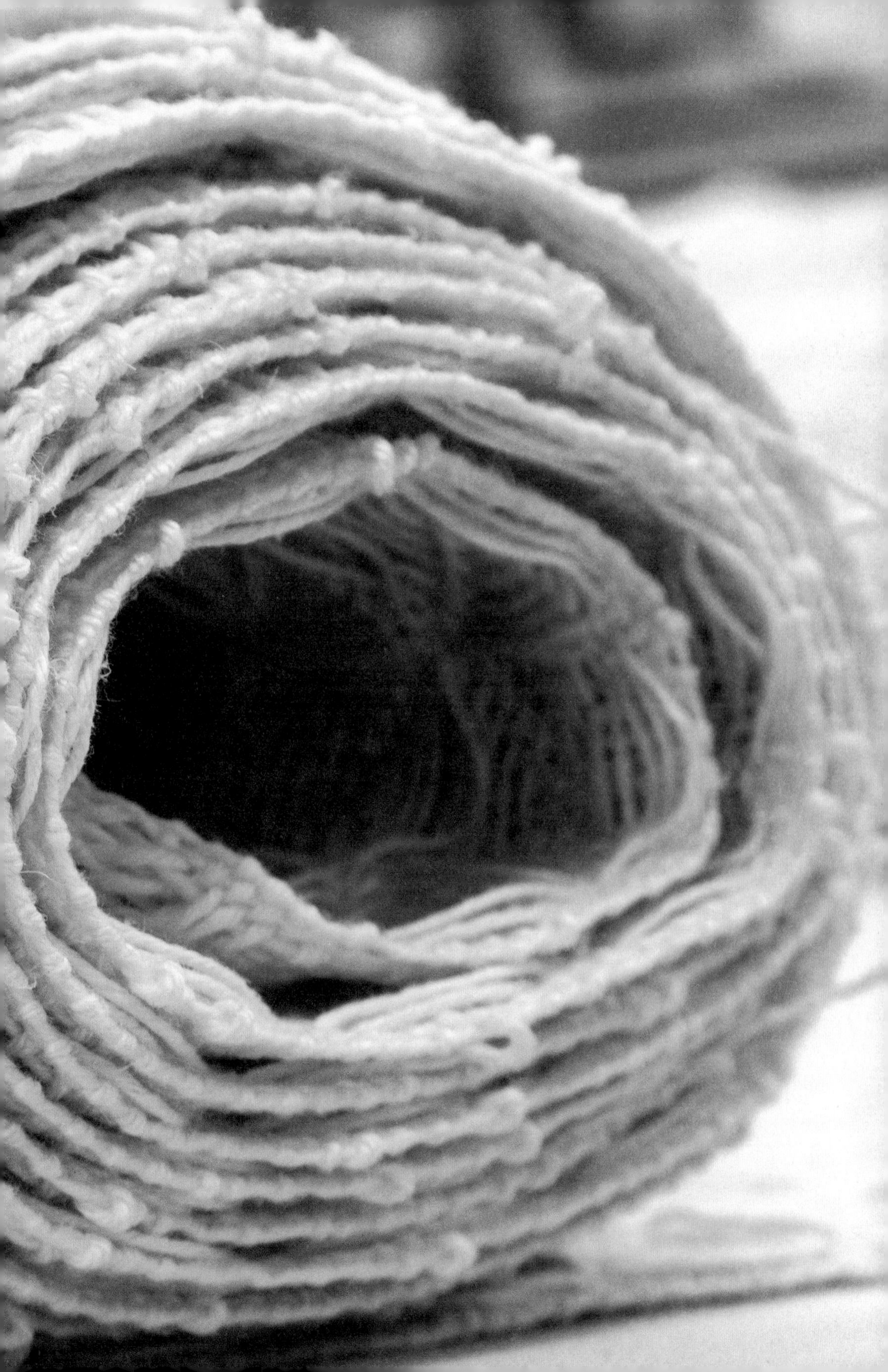

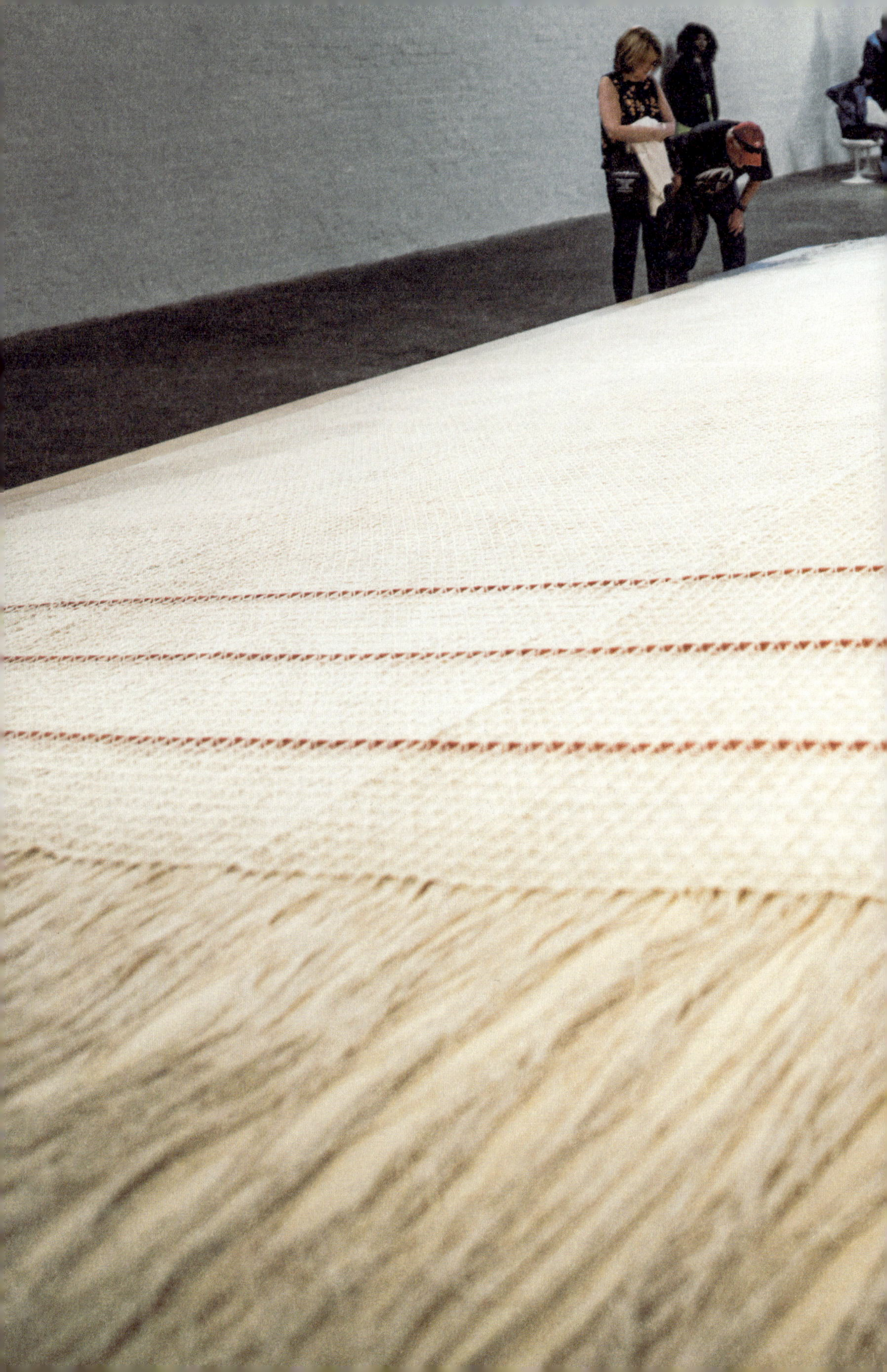

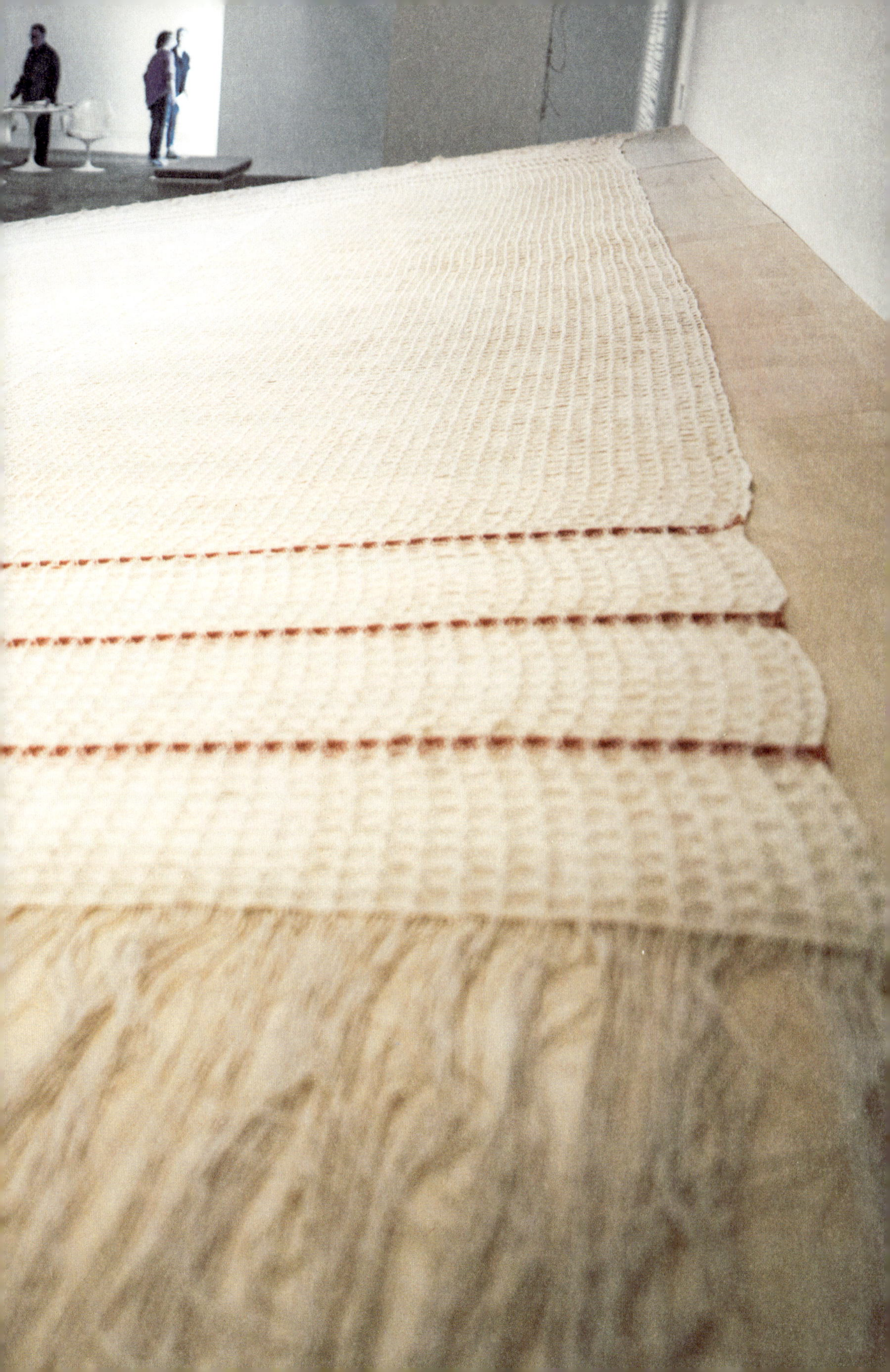

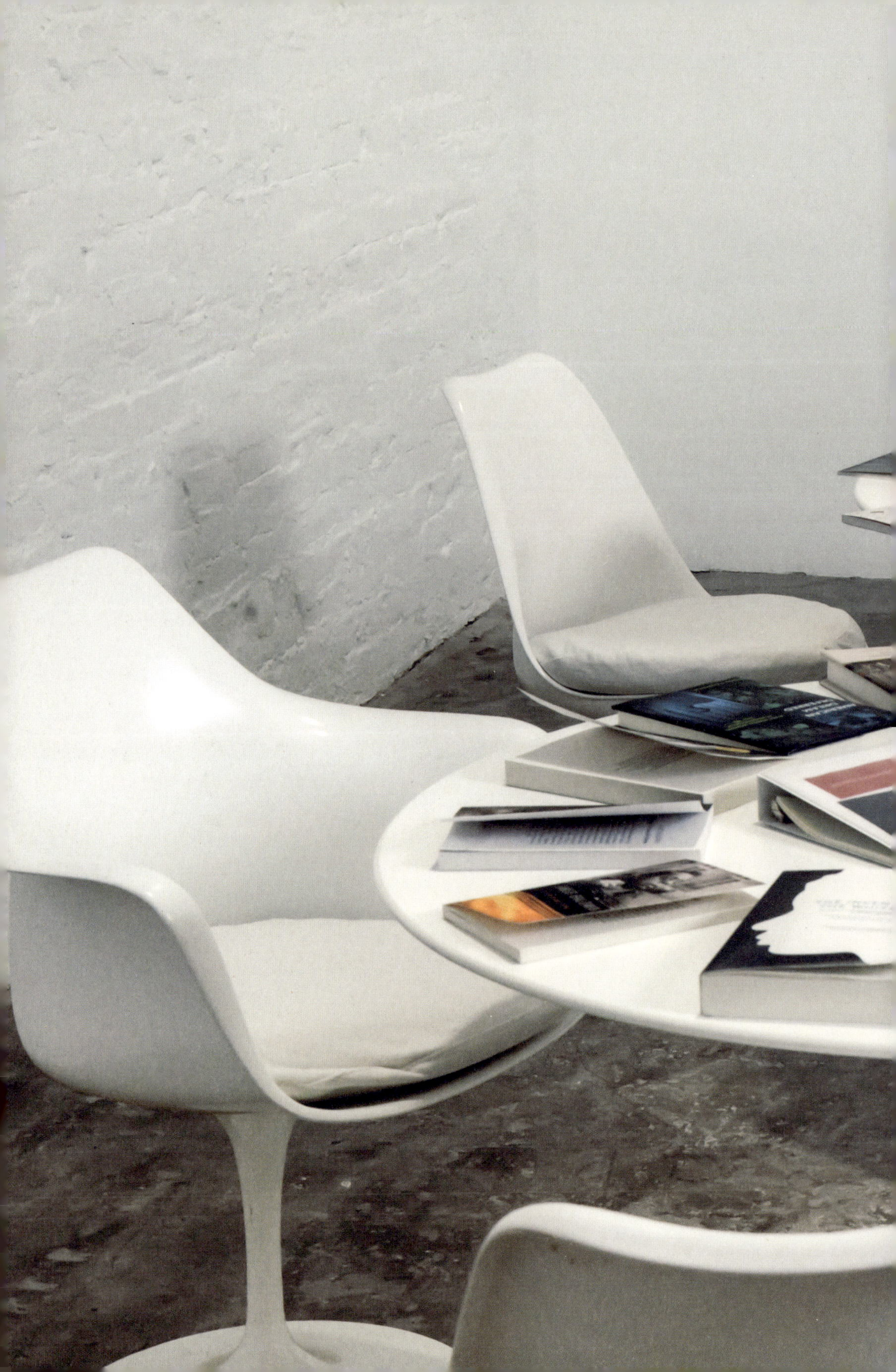

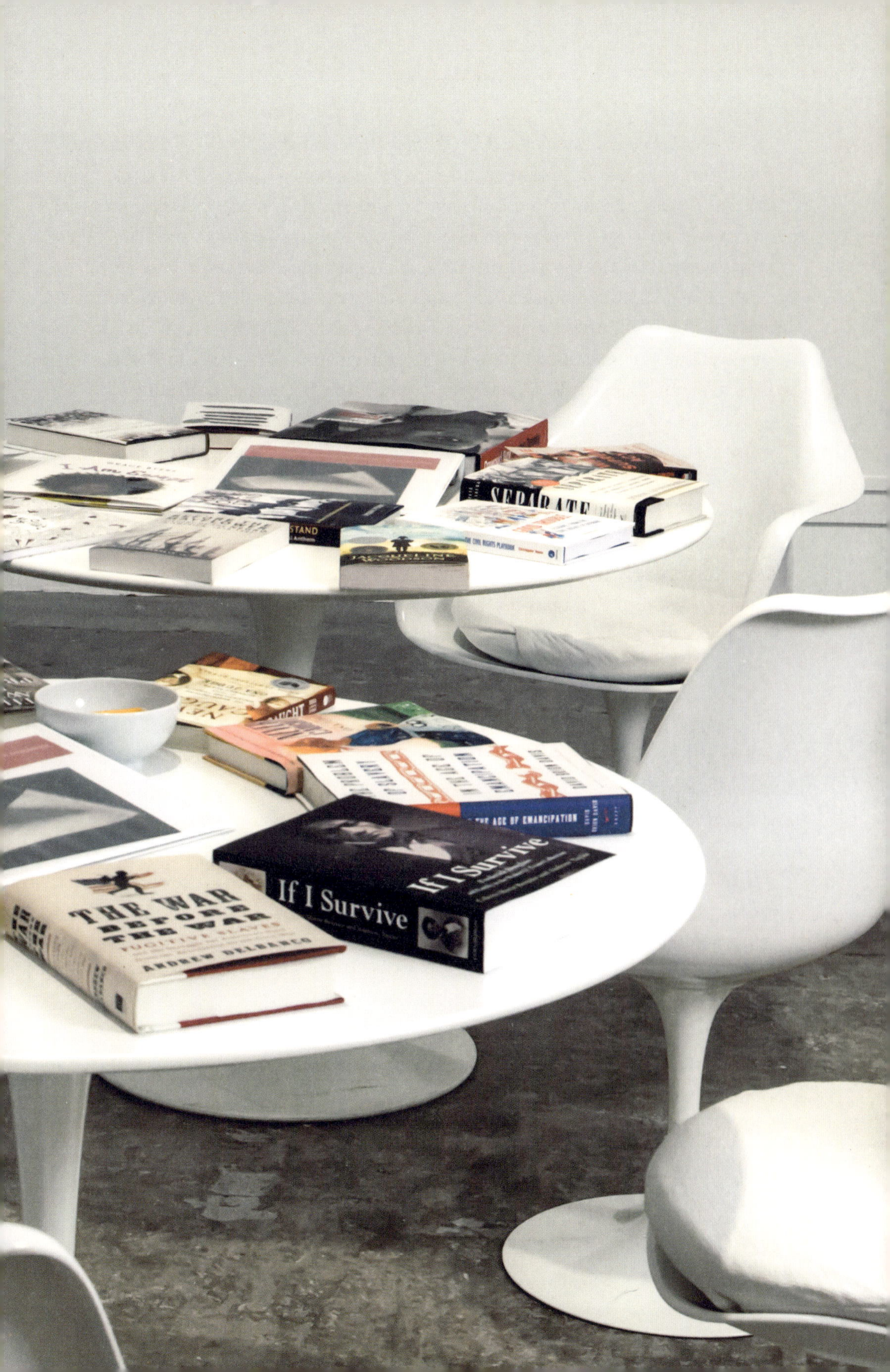

If I Survive
THE WAR BEFORE THE WAR
FUGITIVE SLAVES
ANDREW DELBANCO
SEPARATE
THE AGE OF EMANCIPATION
STAND

that is what creates the symbol that e

dured?

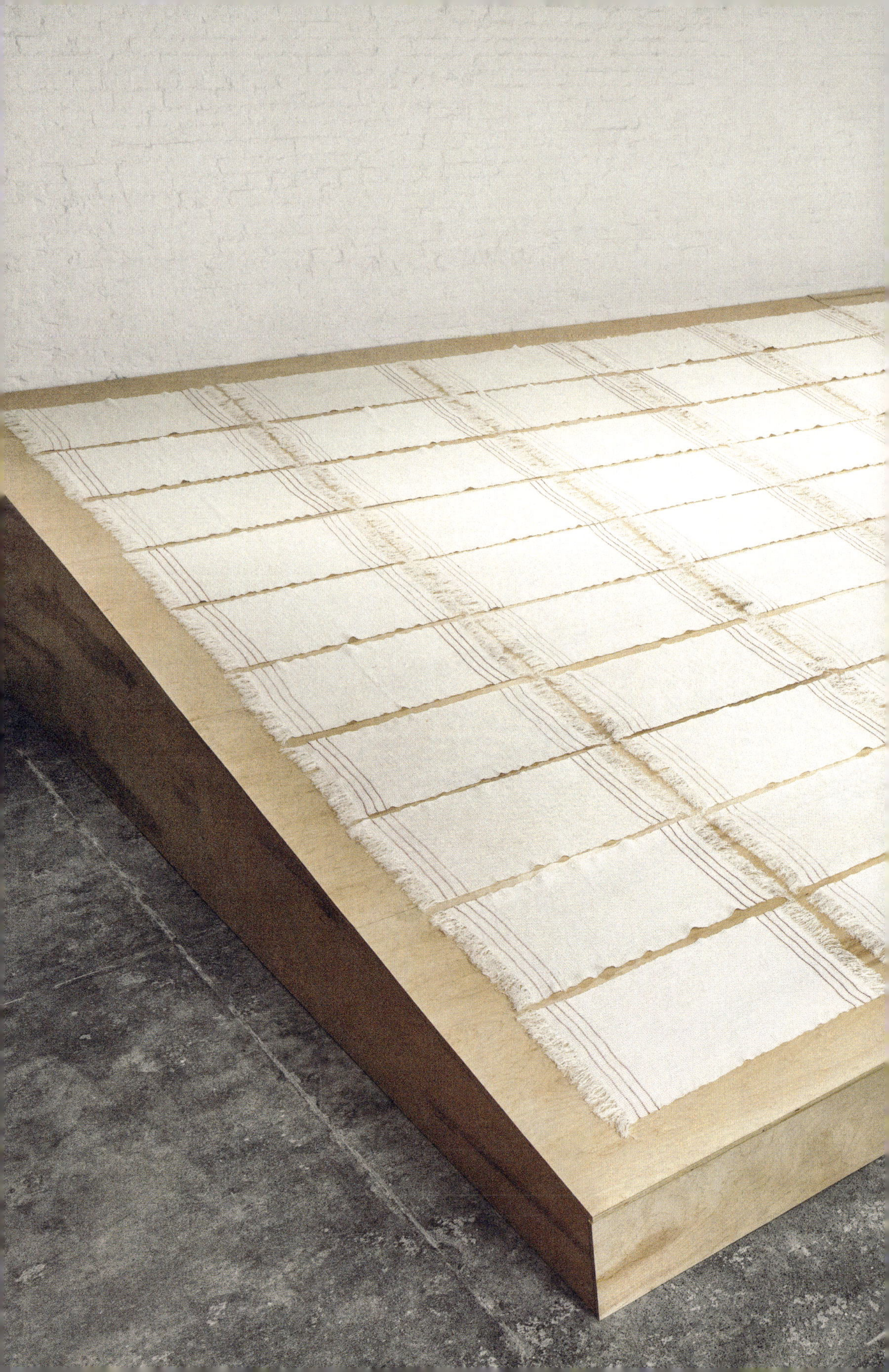

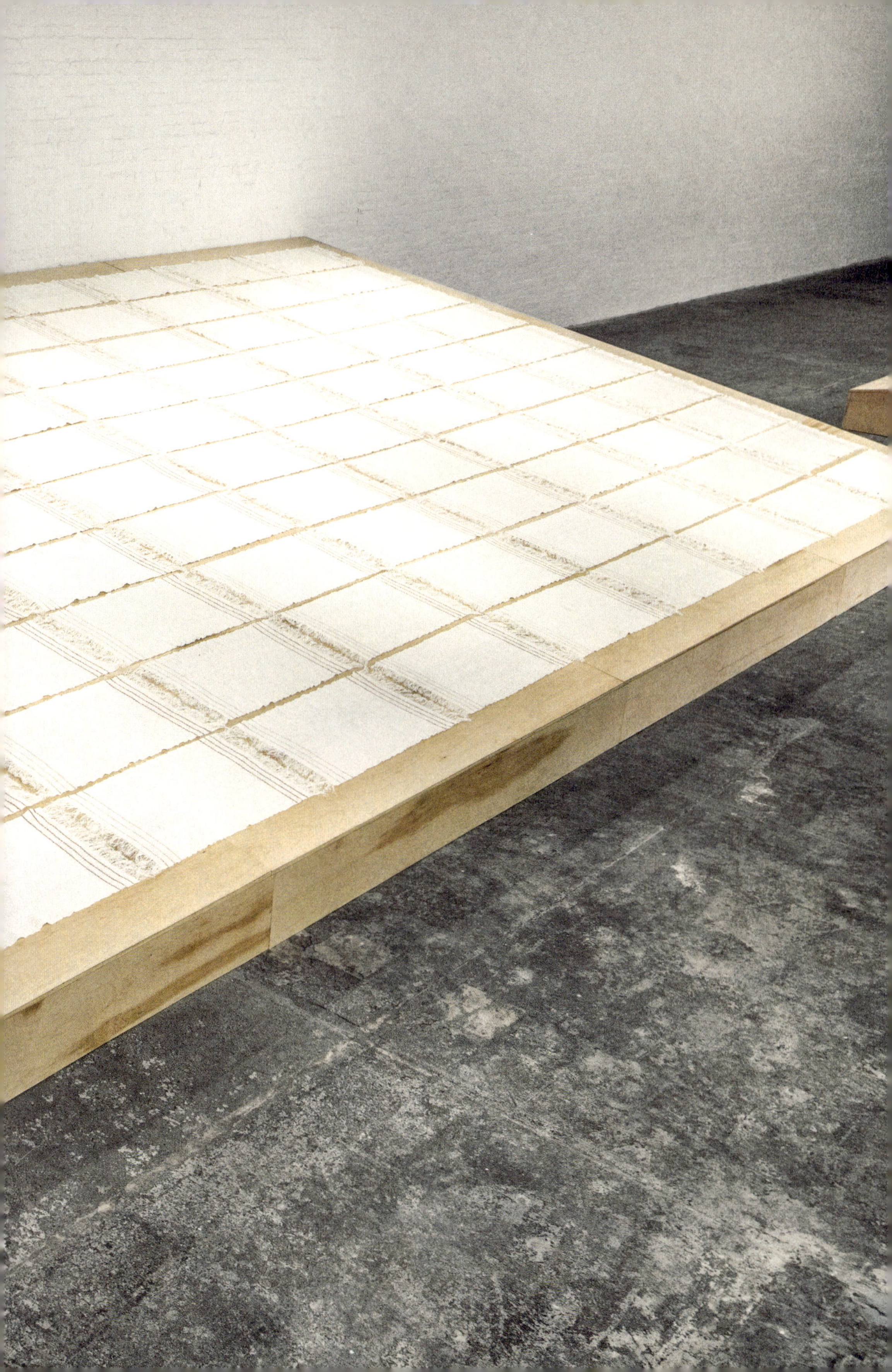

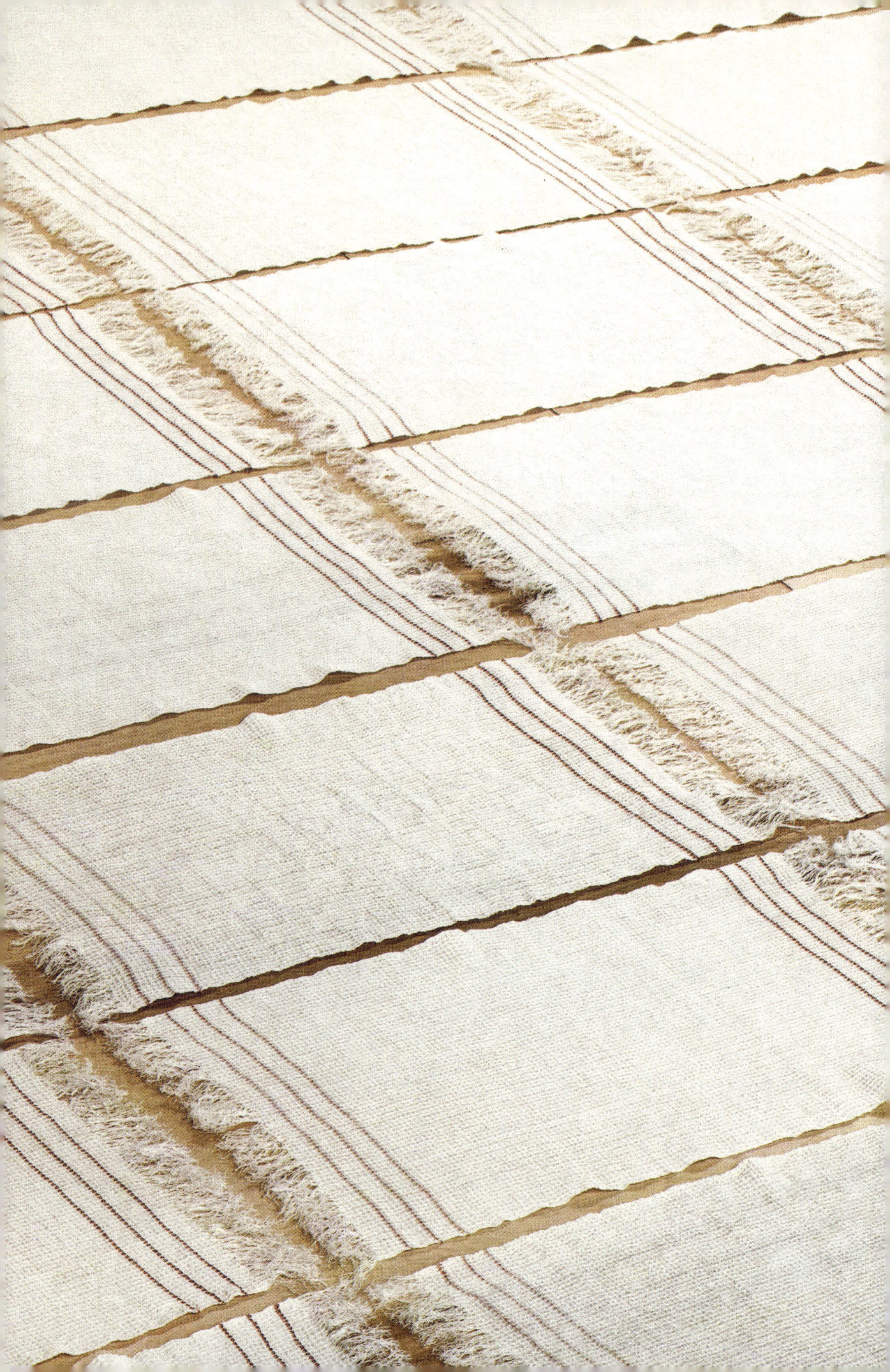

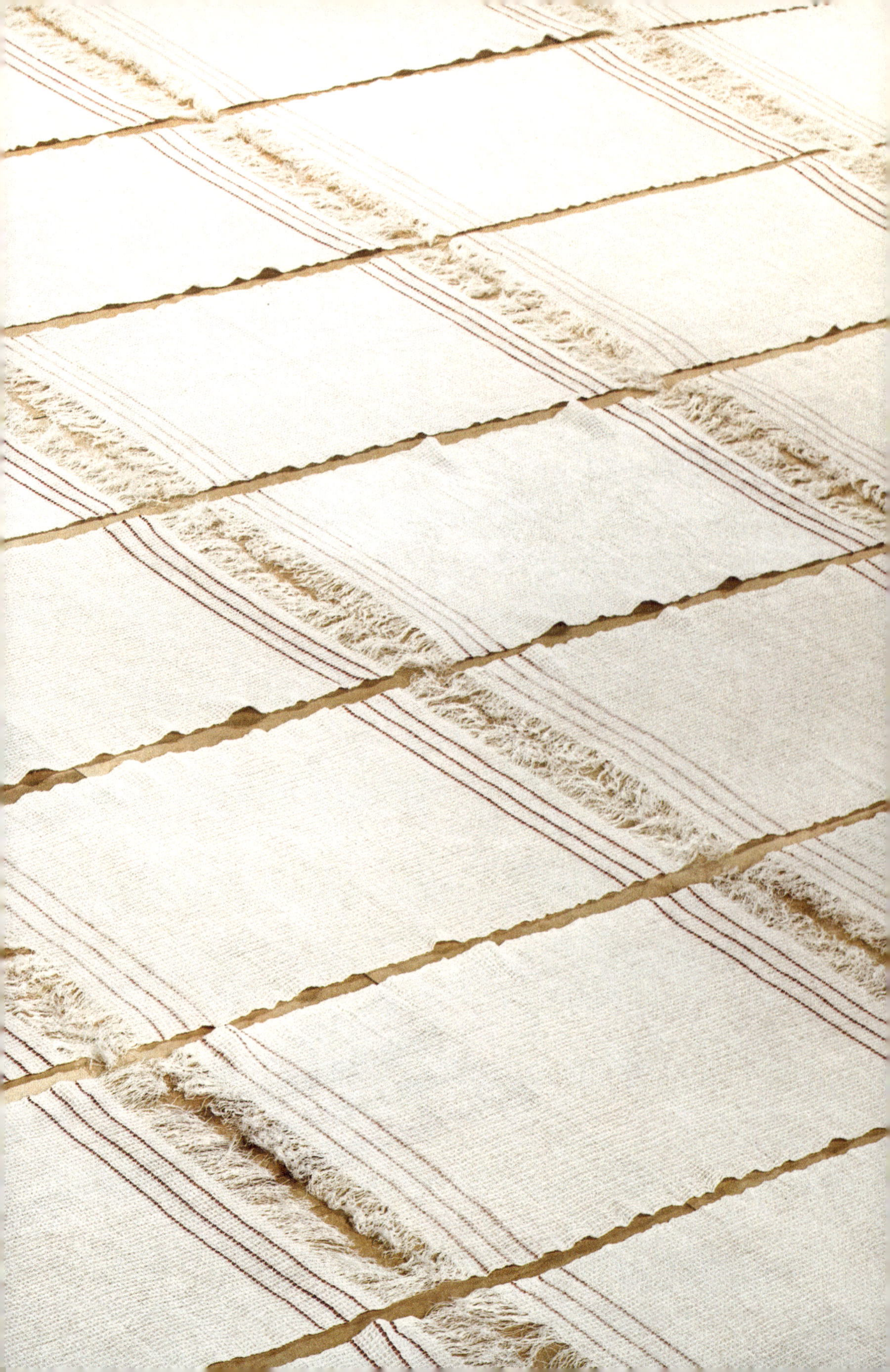

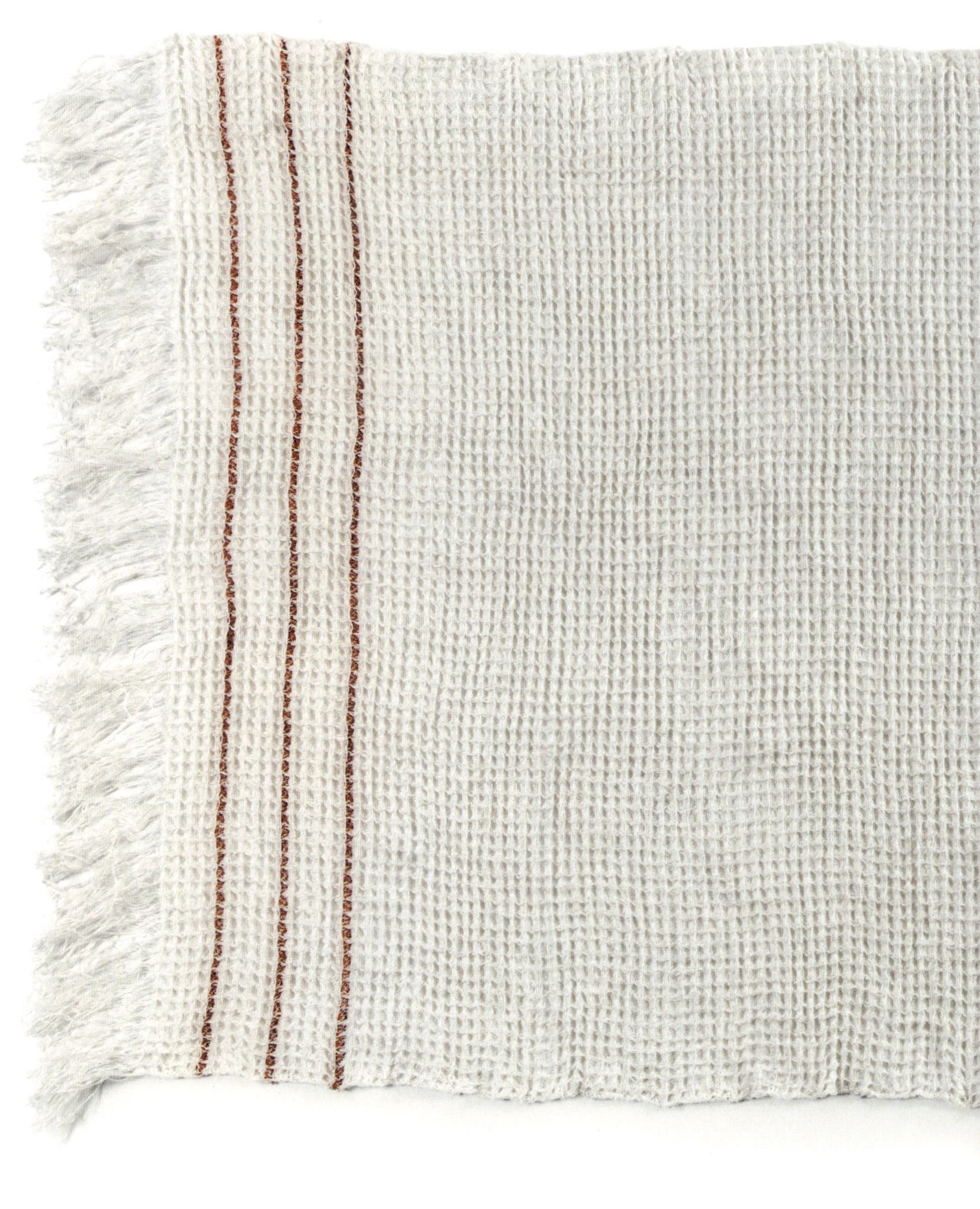

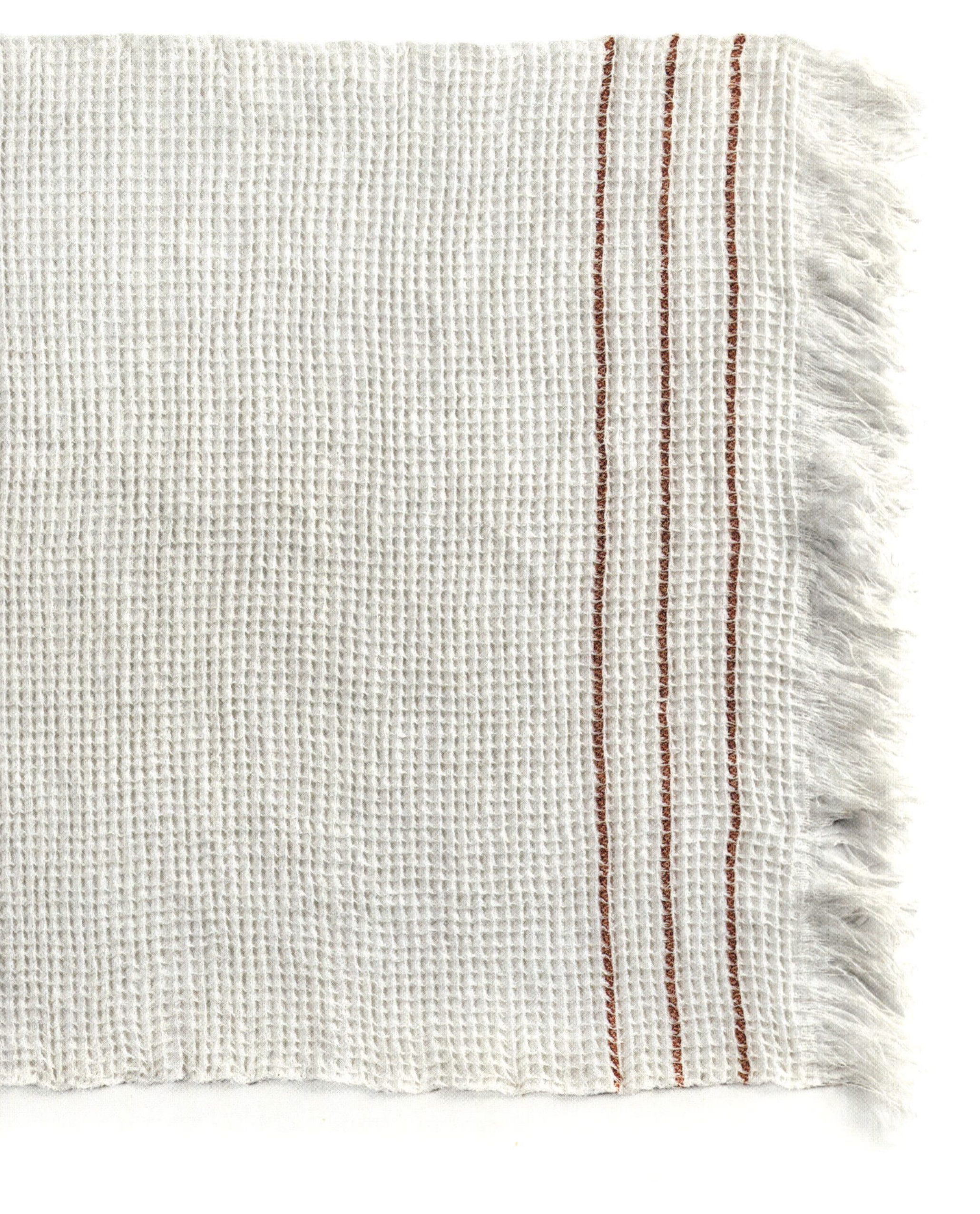

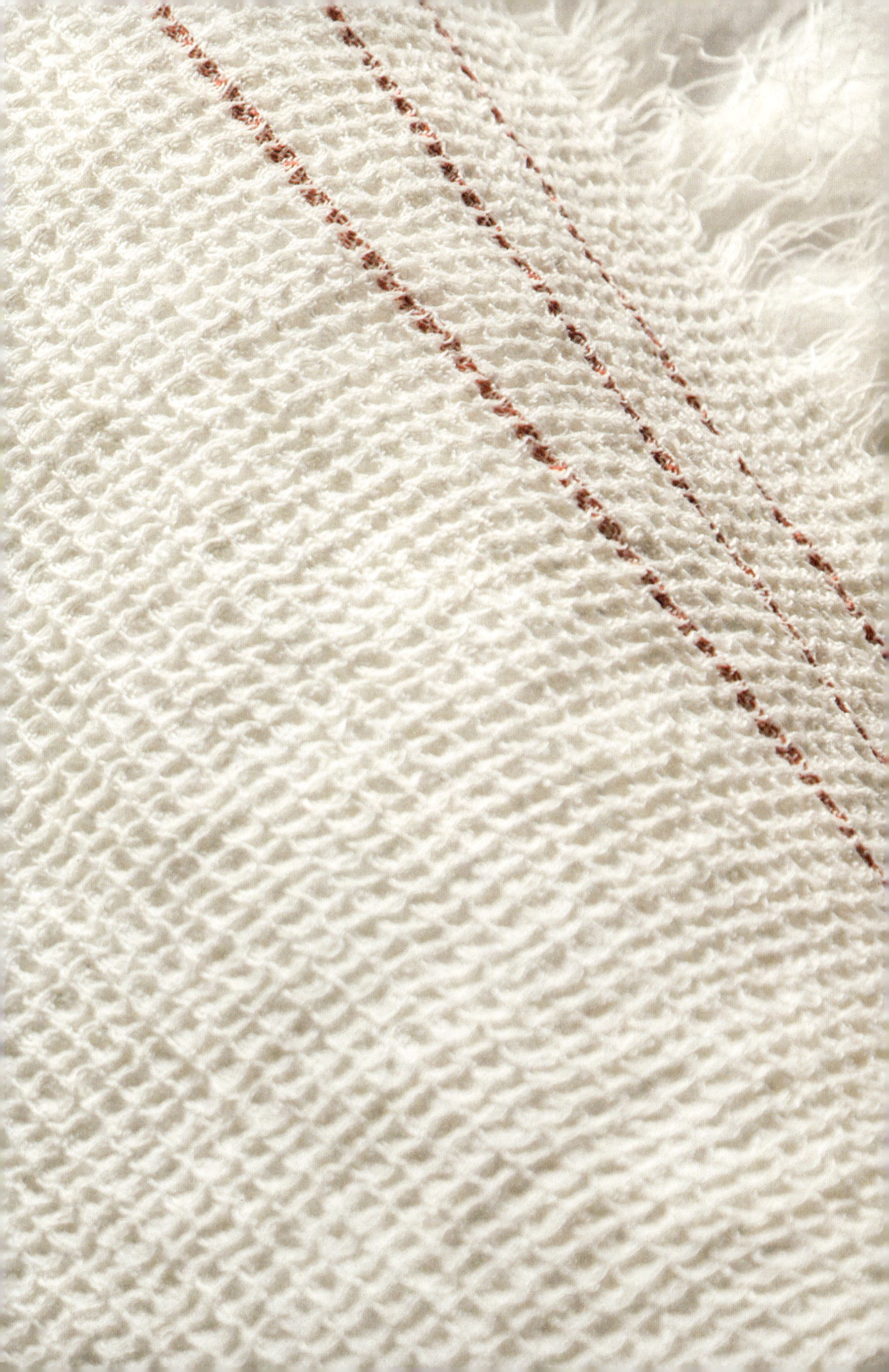

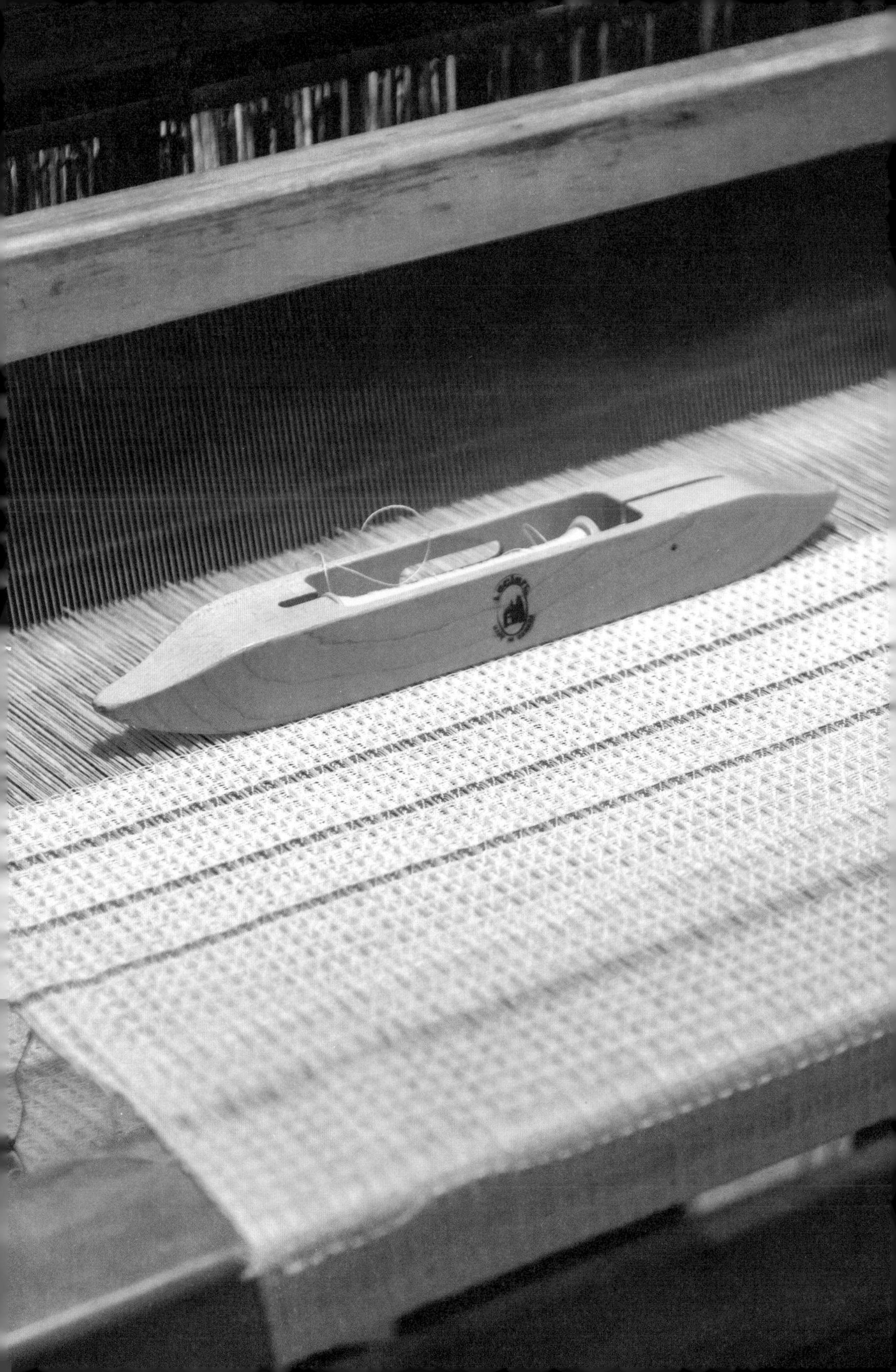

Reconstruction Exercise

The original Confederate Truce Flag was cut into several relics. The largest is in the collection of the National Museum of American History in Washington, D.C. The second-largest portion is at the Appomattox Court House National Historical Park in Virginia. The Truce Flag, the same cloth that held the promise of bringing the nation back together after the Civil War, was divided. Issues requiring resolution at the end of the Civil War—reconciliation, racial justice, and civil rights—continue to plague the nation today.

Reconstruction Exercise is one of two participatory installations. The audience is invited to learn about this symbolic artifact by weaving its complex waffle-weave structure on looms similar to those used to make the original Truce Flag. Each participant constructs a portion of what will become one of nine elongated truce flags. These textiles are akin to scrolls. Collaboratively created by novices and experienced weavers, the finished textiles document a range of skill levels, from struggle to mastery, in reconstructing this emblem of surrender, truce, peace, and reconciliation.

Reconstruction Exercise, 2019. Nine floor looms, benches, and linen. Dimensions variable. In collaboration with The Fabric Workshop and Museum, Philadelphia

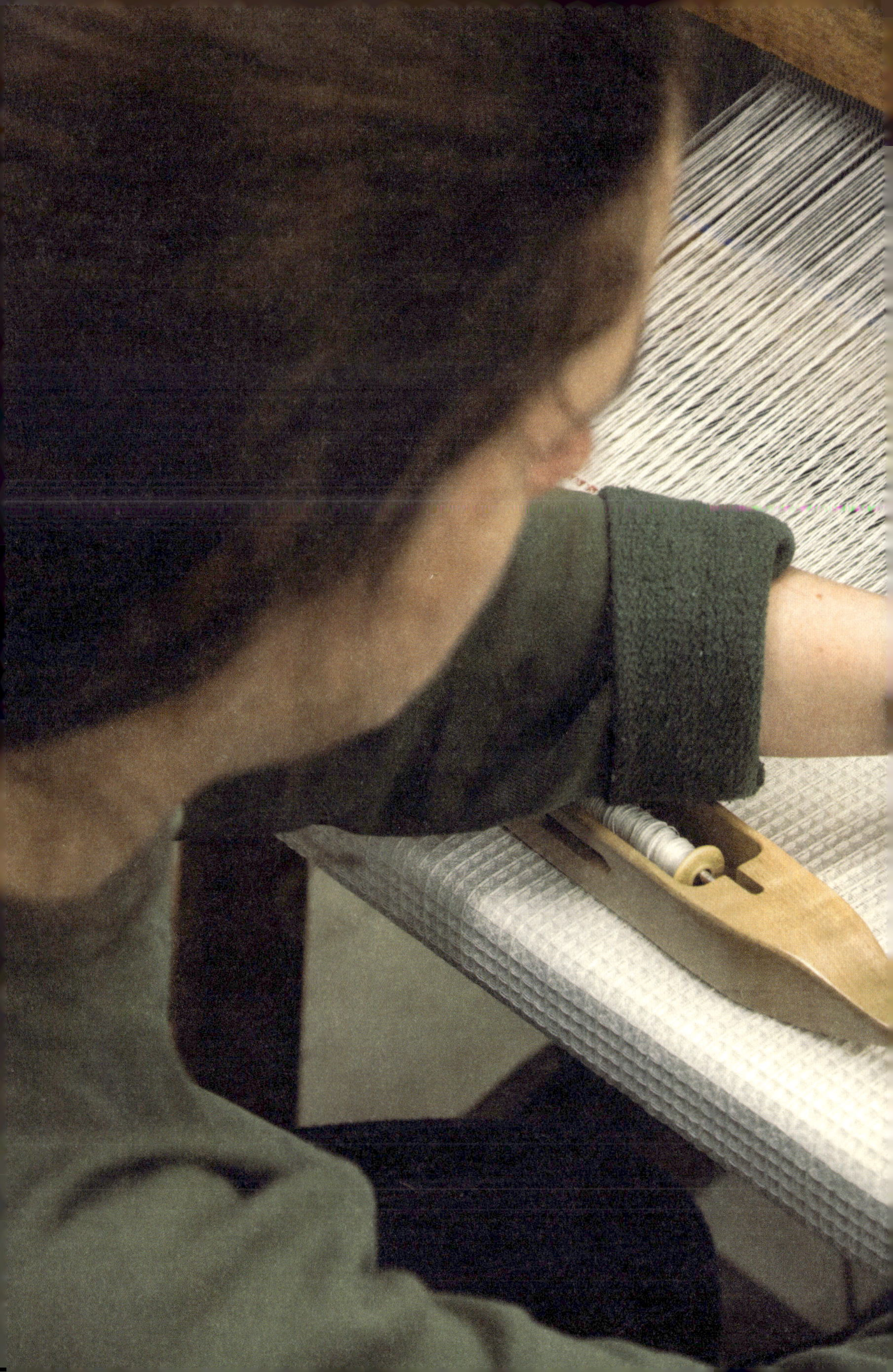

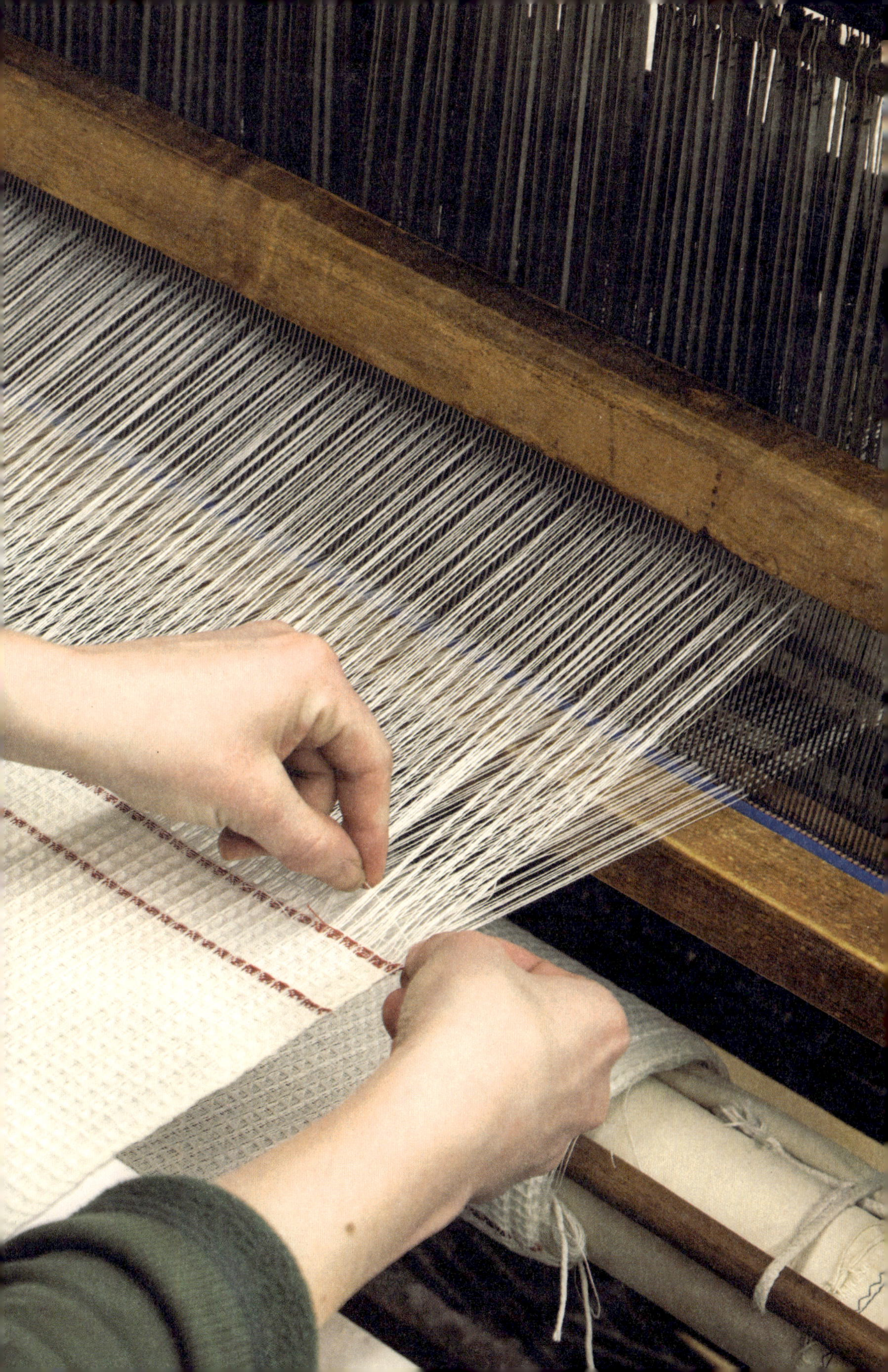

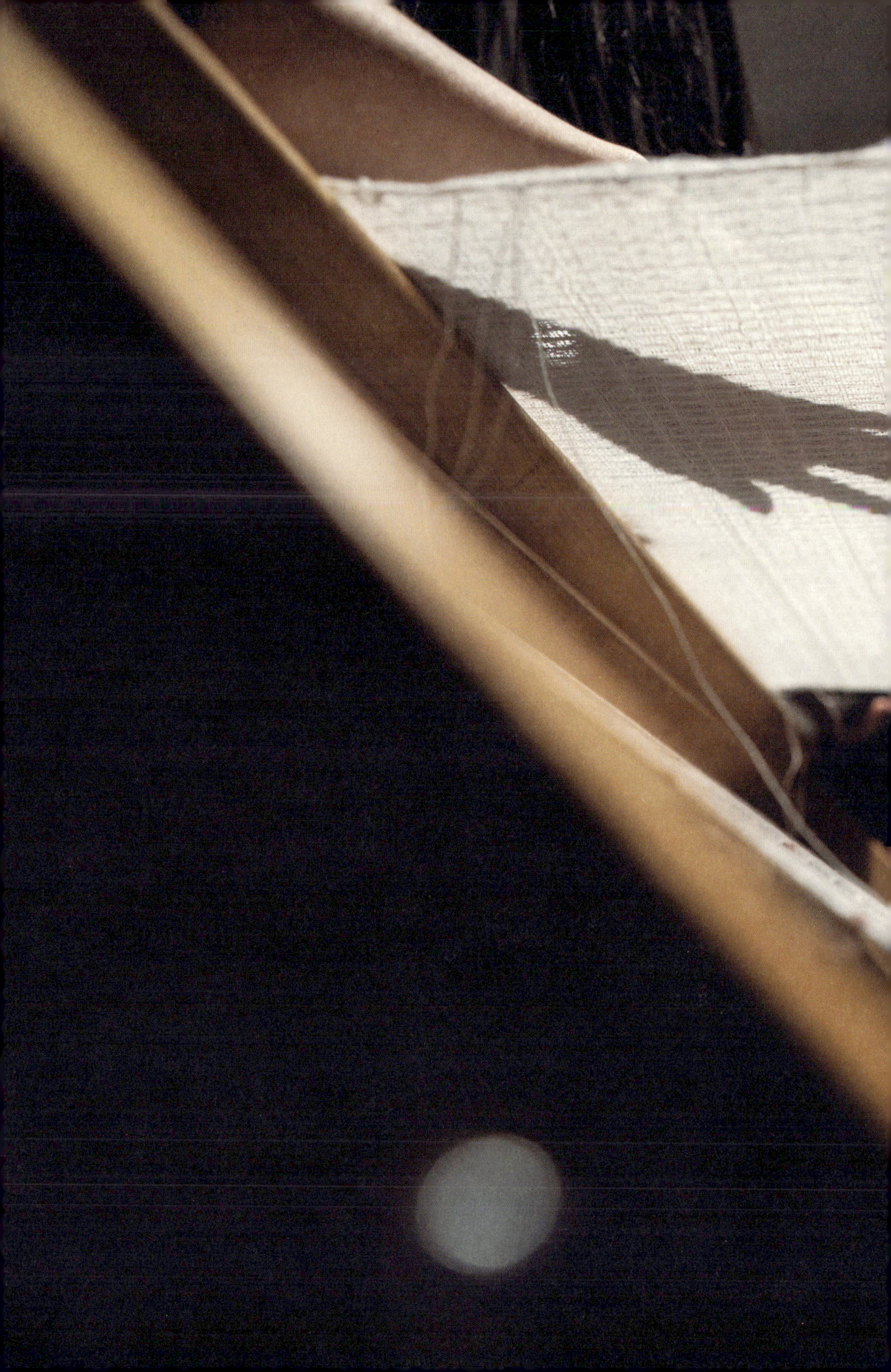

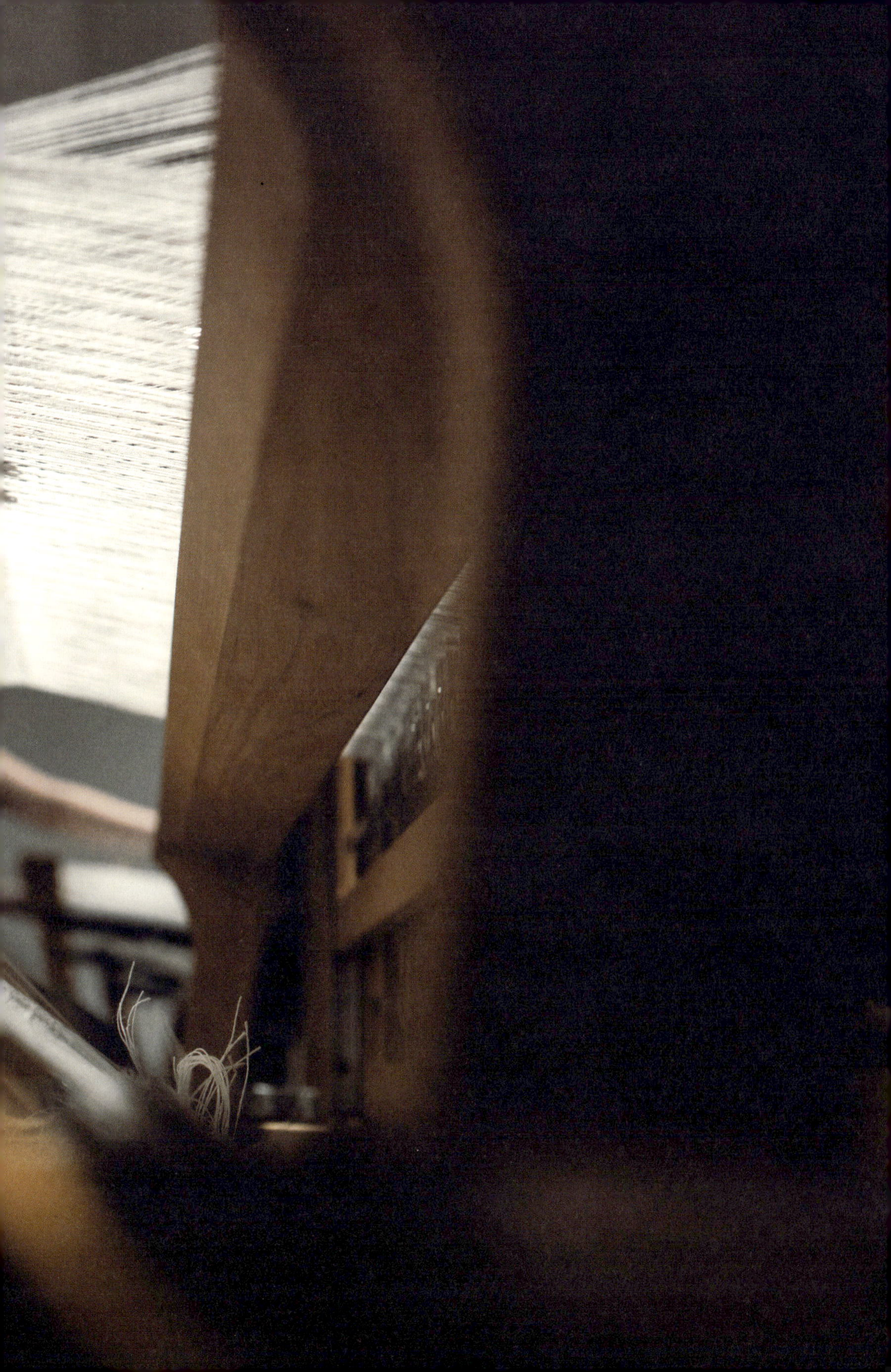

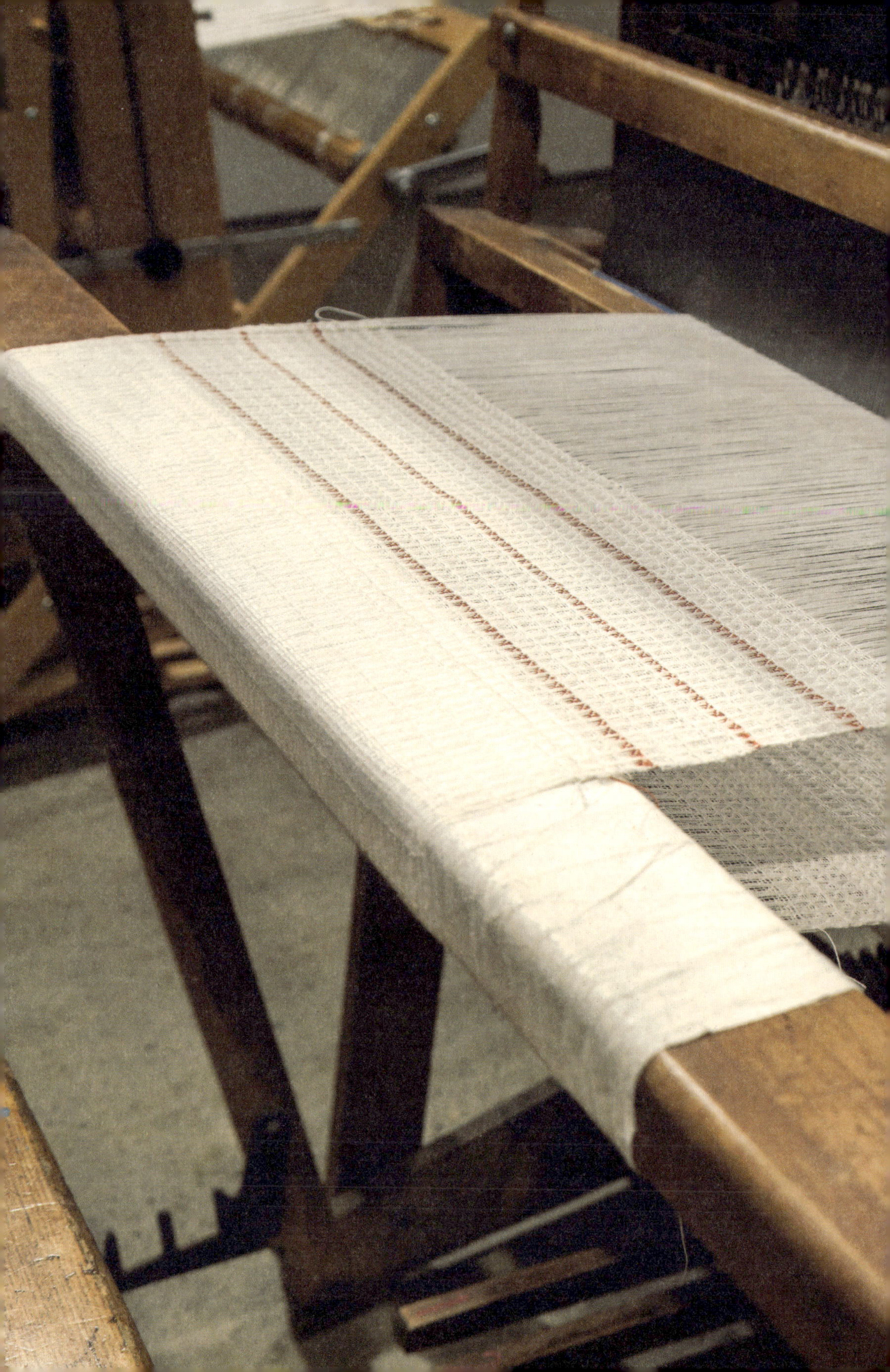

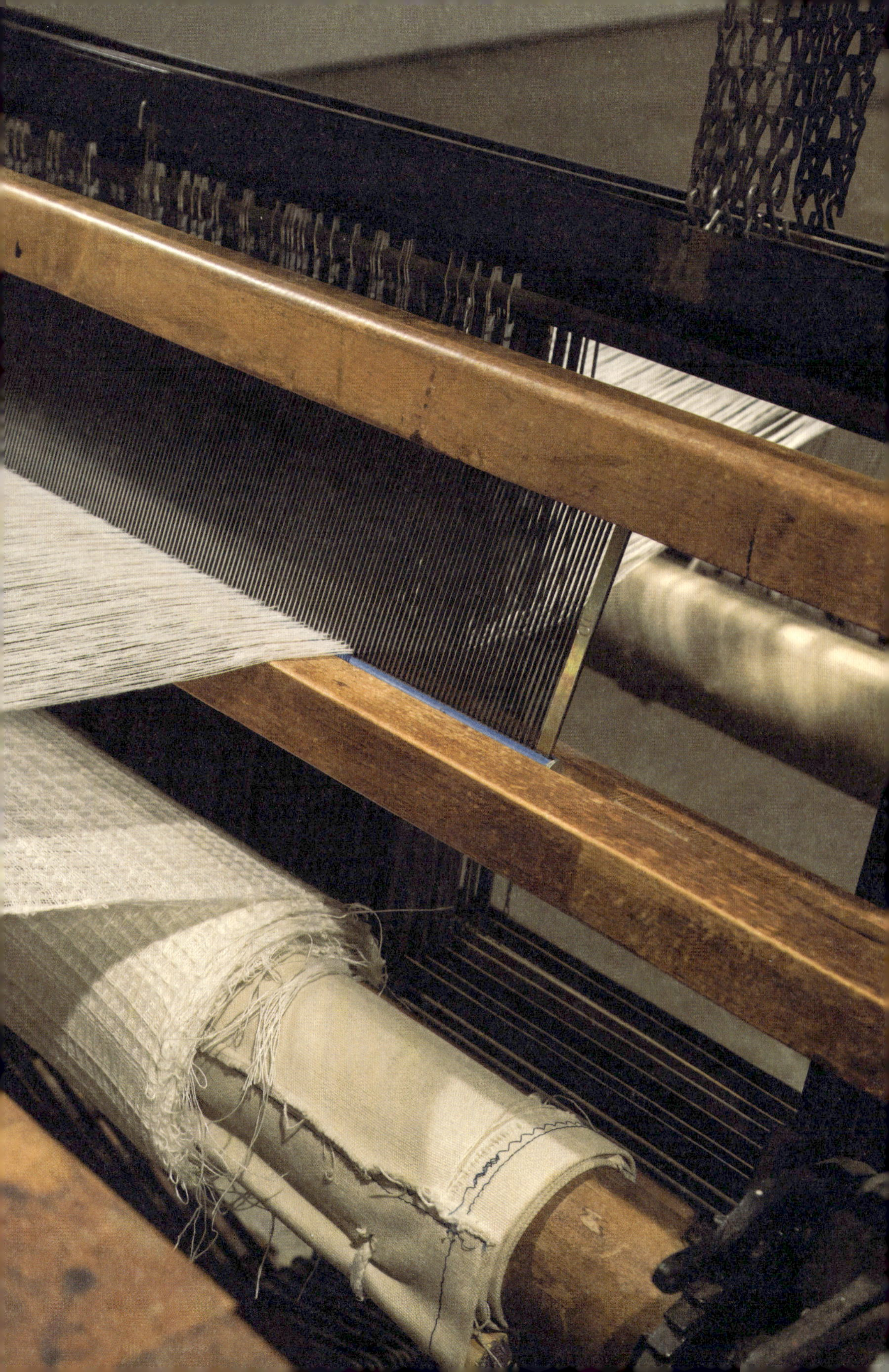

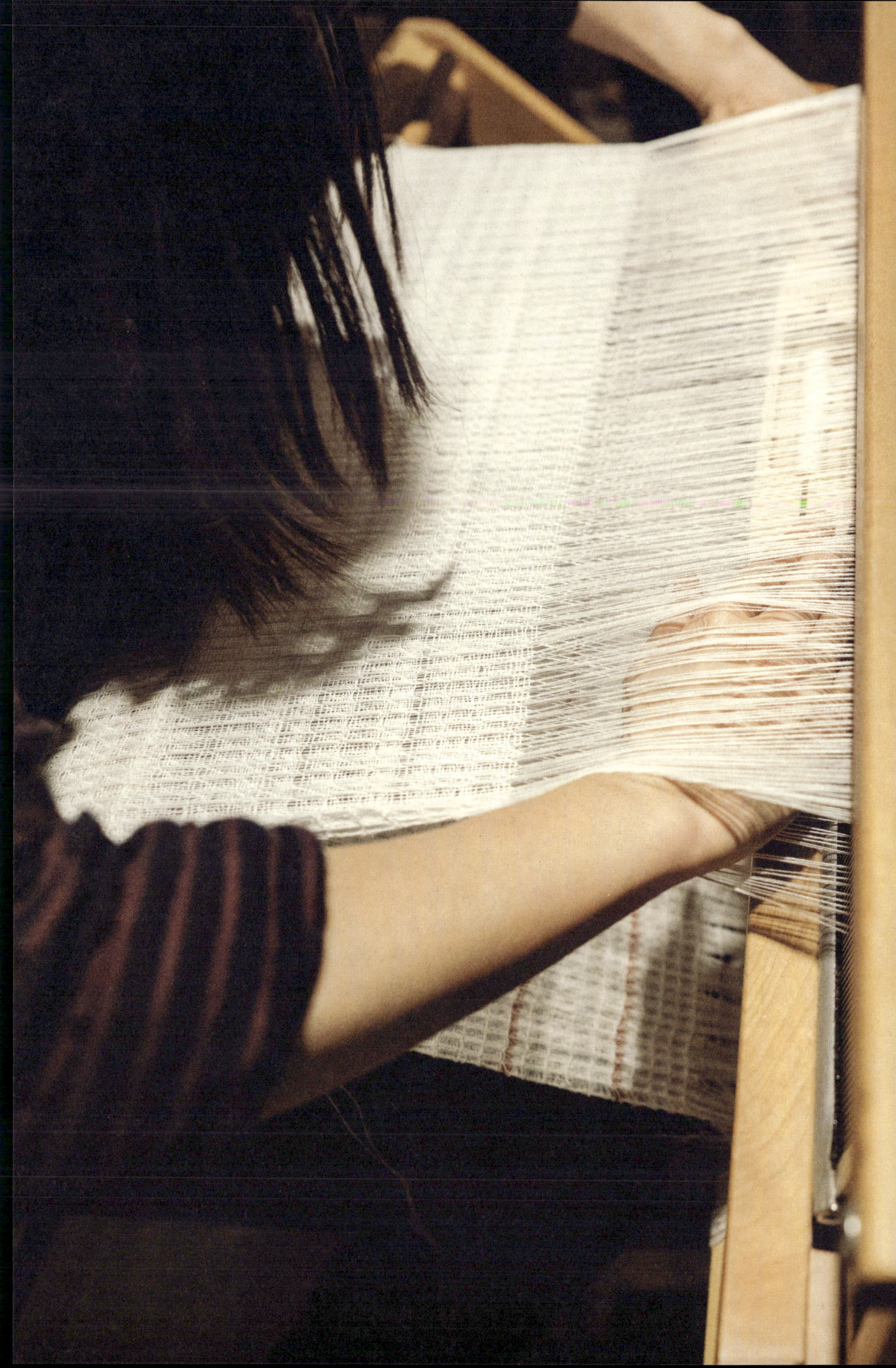

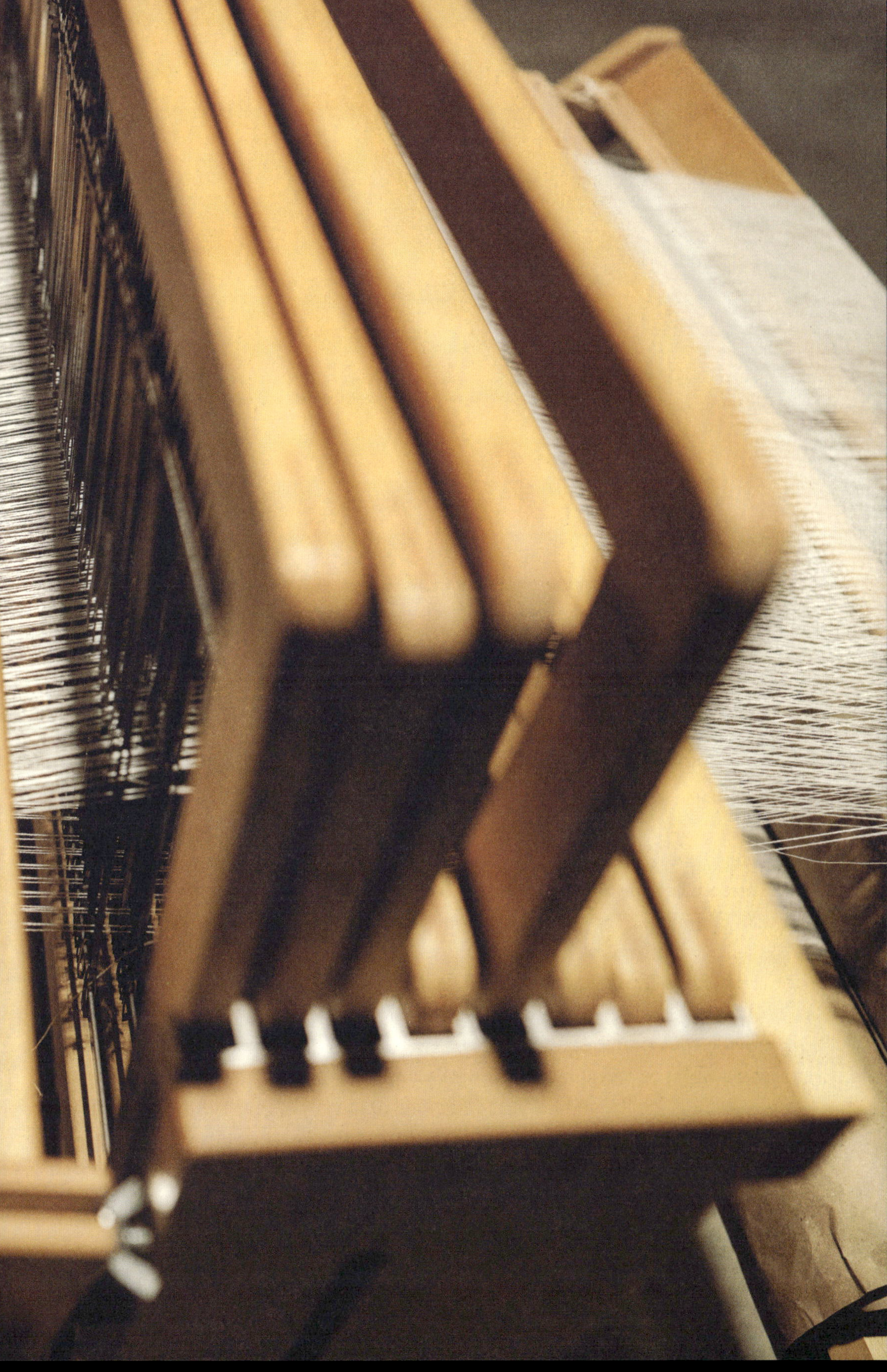

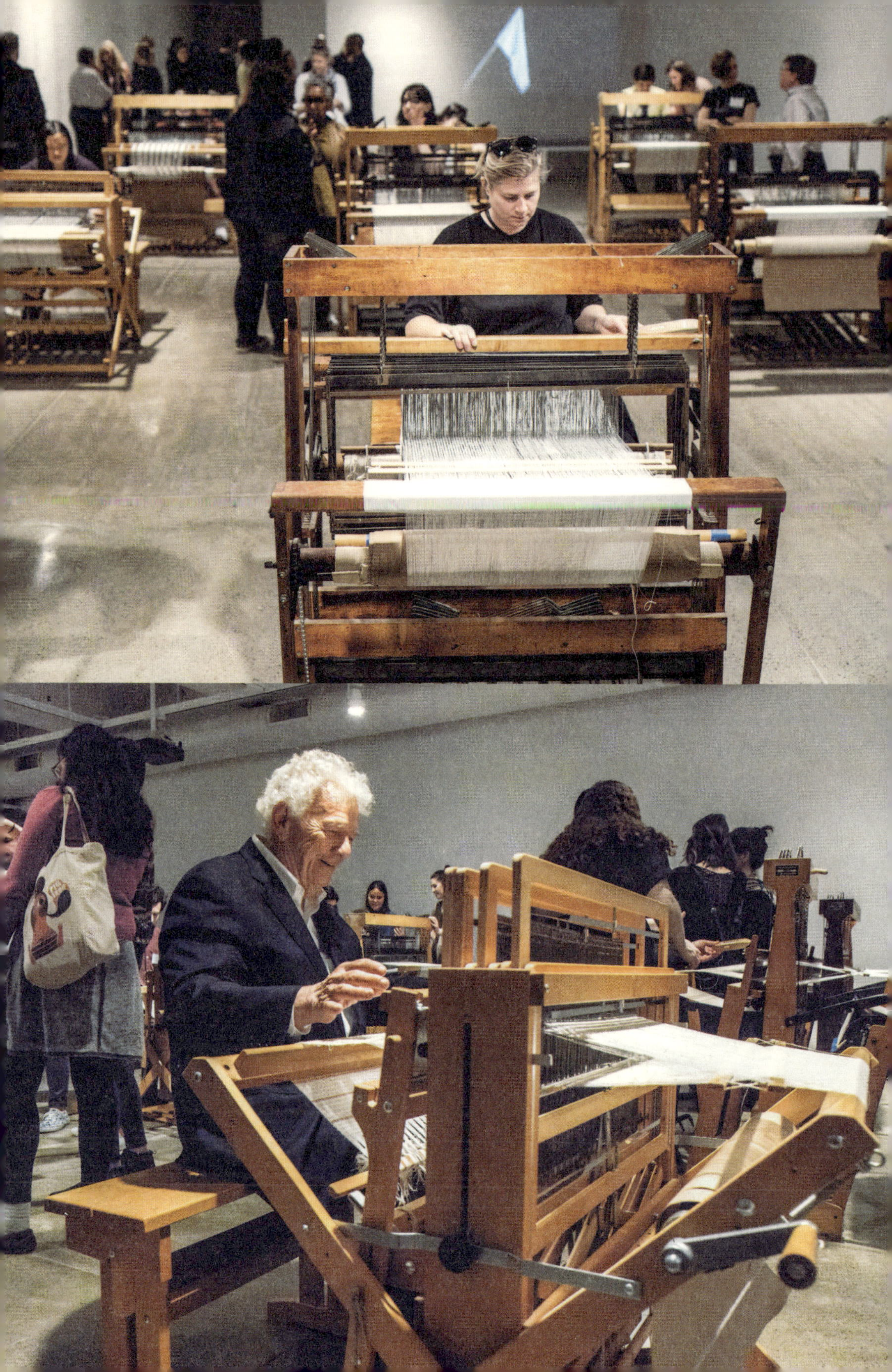

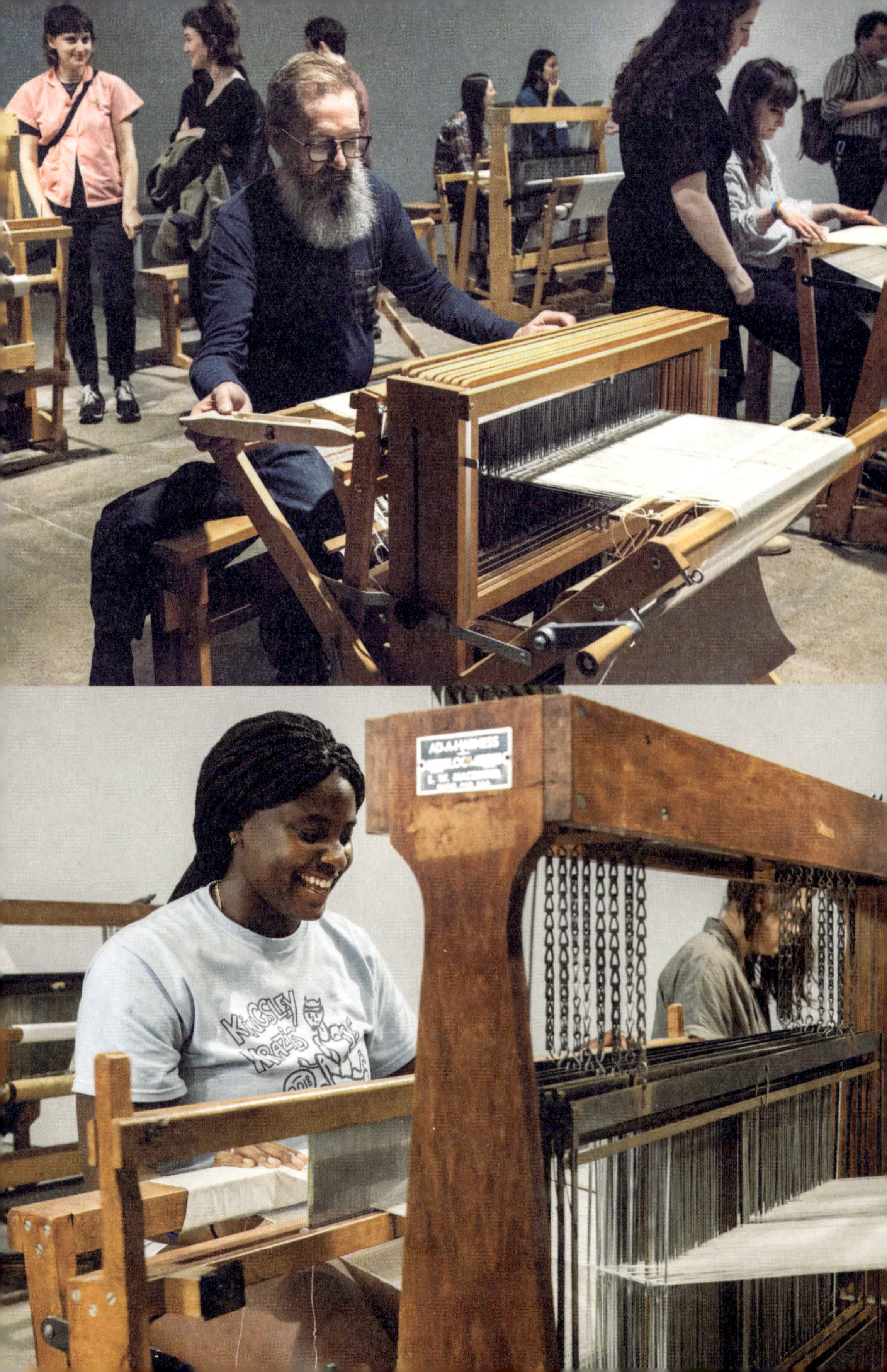

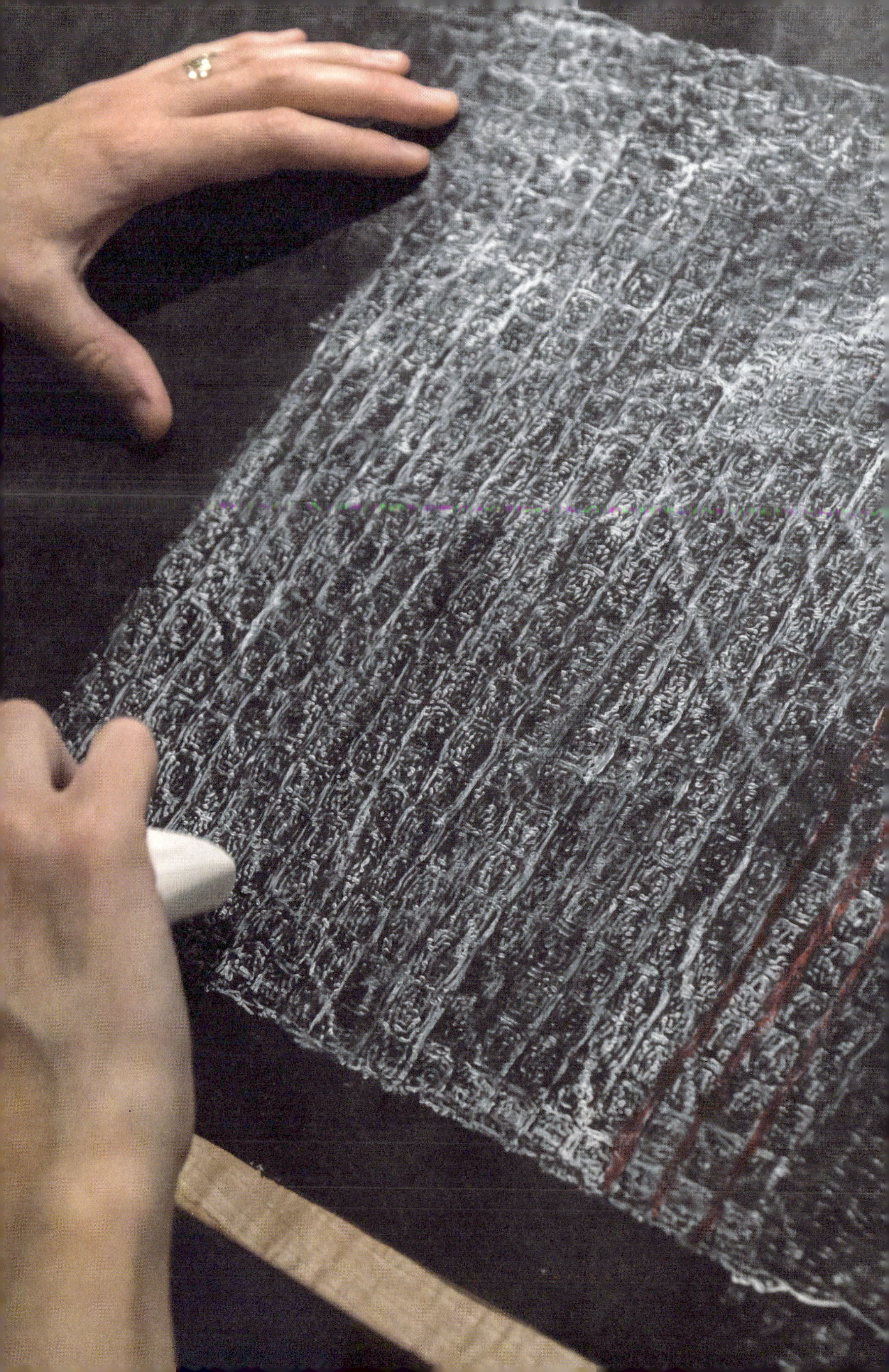

Lesson Plan (Confederate Truce Flag)

A domestic cloth—a dishcloth, likely similar to those found in many homes at the time of the Civil War and even today—was elevated to historical status when it was re-purposed as a truce flag to initiate the end of the war in 1865. It was not designed to be a flag. It became the Confederate Truce Flag because it had the necessary property of a truce flag, namely, that it was predominantly white. But this dishcloth also had a specific texture (a waffle weave), minimal design elements (three thin red stripes on either end), and a fringe. All these elements help to identify this particular flag and transform it into a symbol.

Lesson Plan engages the audience in reproducing the texture and design of the Truce Flag. Participants sit at historical school desks, each retrofitted with a laser-etched image of the Truce Flag, and use white crayons to make rubbings of the cloth's texture on pieces of black Tyvek. Red crayons are provided to make the three lines on either end of the rubbing, replicating the design of the original. Visitors can take their creations with them to disseminate knowledge about the Truce Flag and inspire further reflection about the symbols and monuments that are present in our daily lives.

Lesson Plan (Confederate Truce Flag), 2019. Nine school desks with a laser-etched image of the Truce Flag, Tyvek, and white and red crayons. Dimensions variable. In collaboration with The Fabric Workshop and Museum, Philadelphia

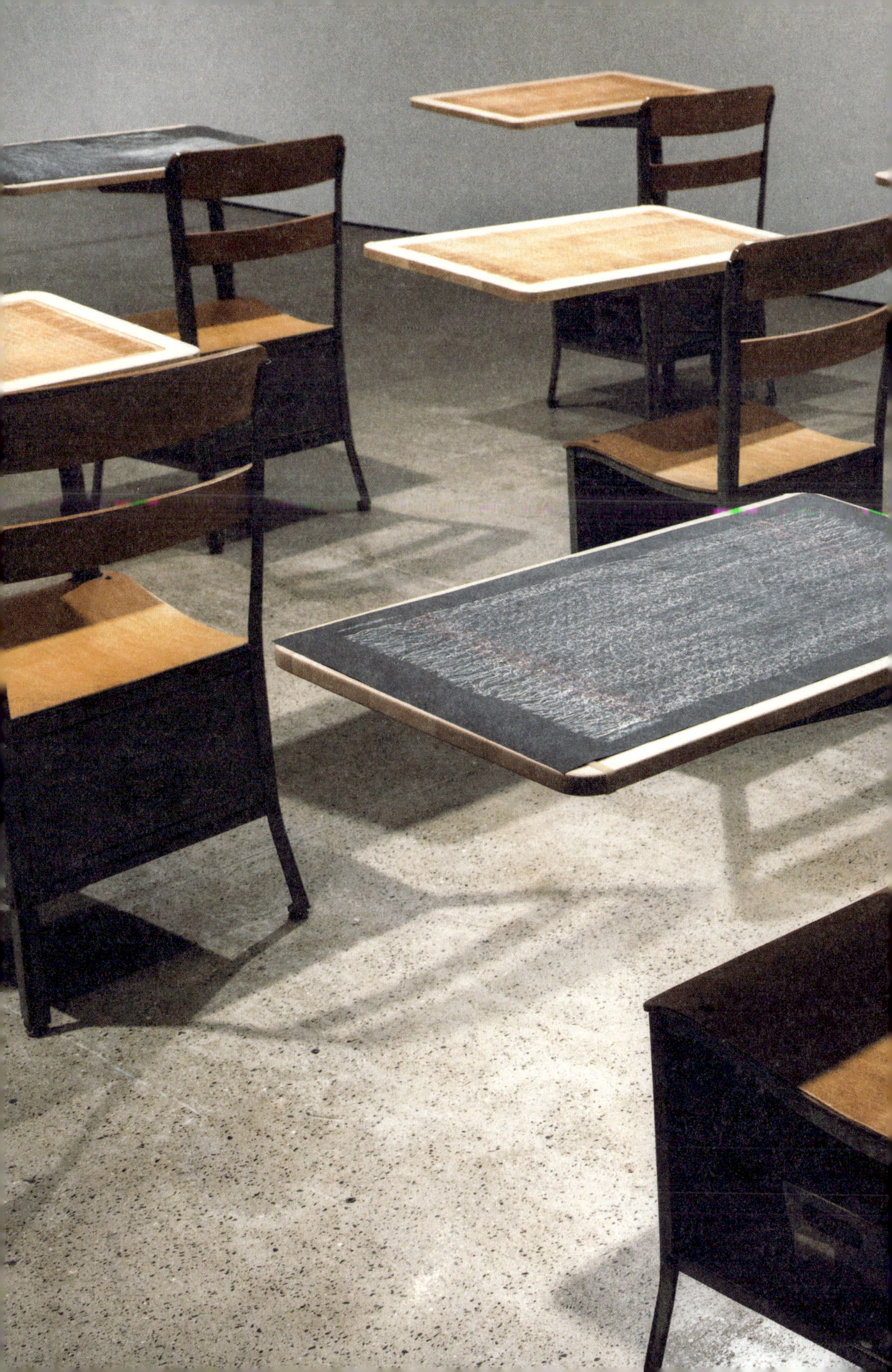

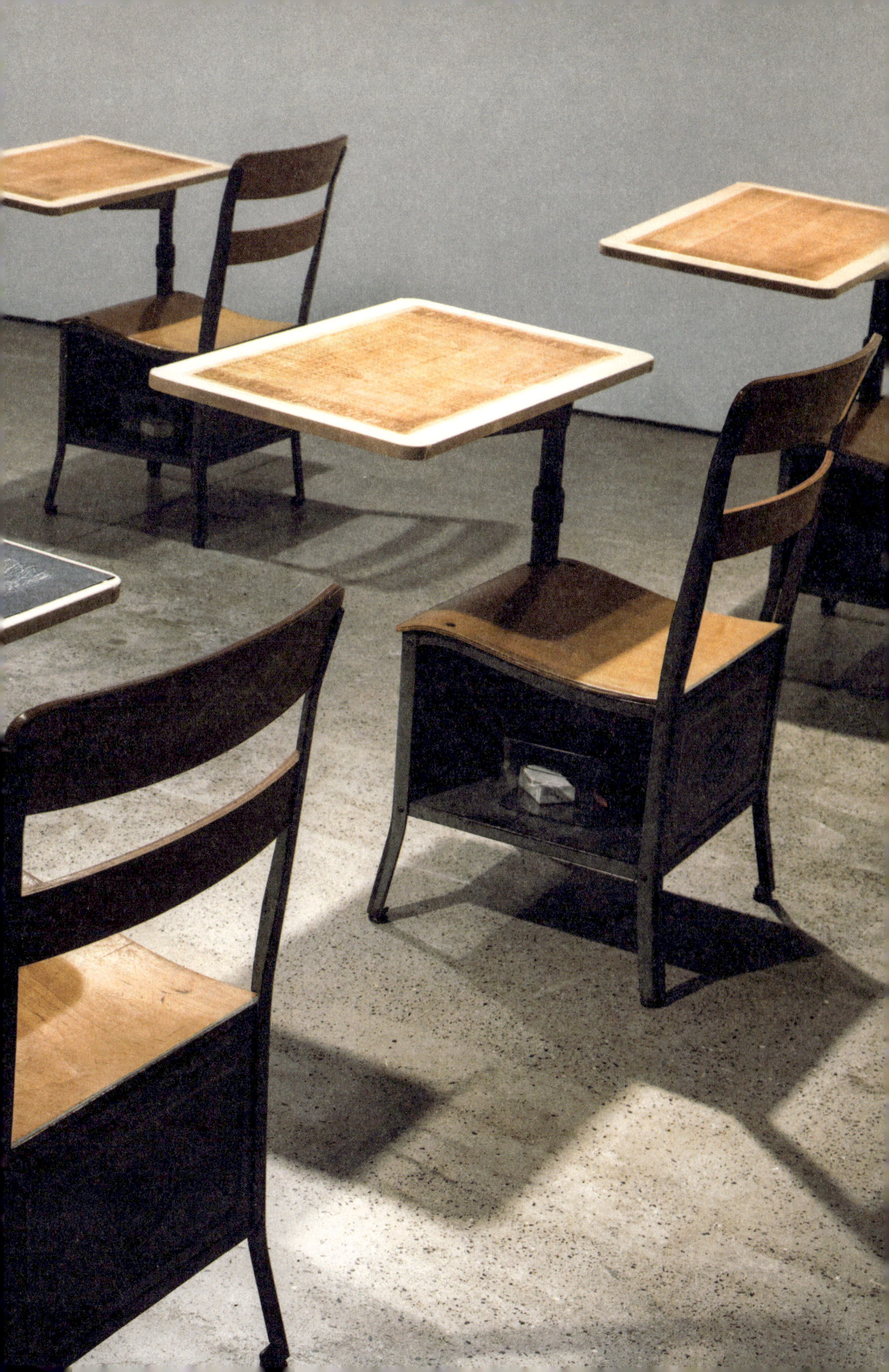

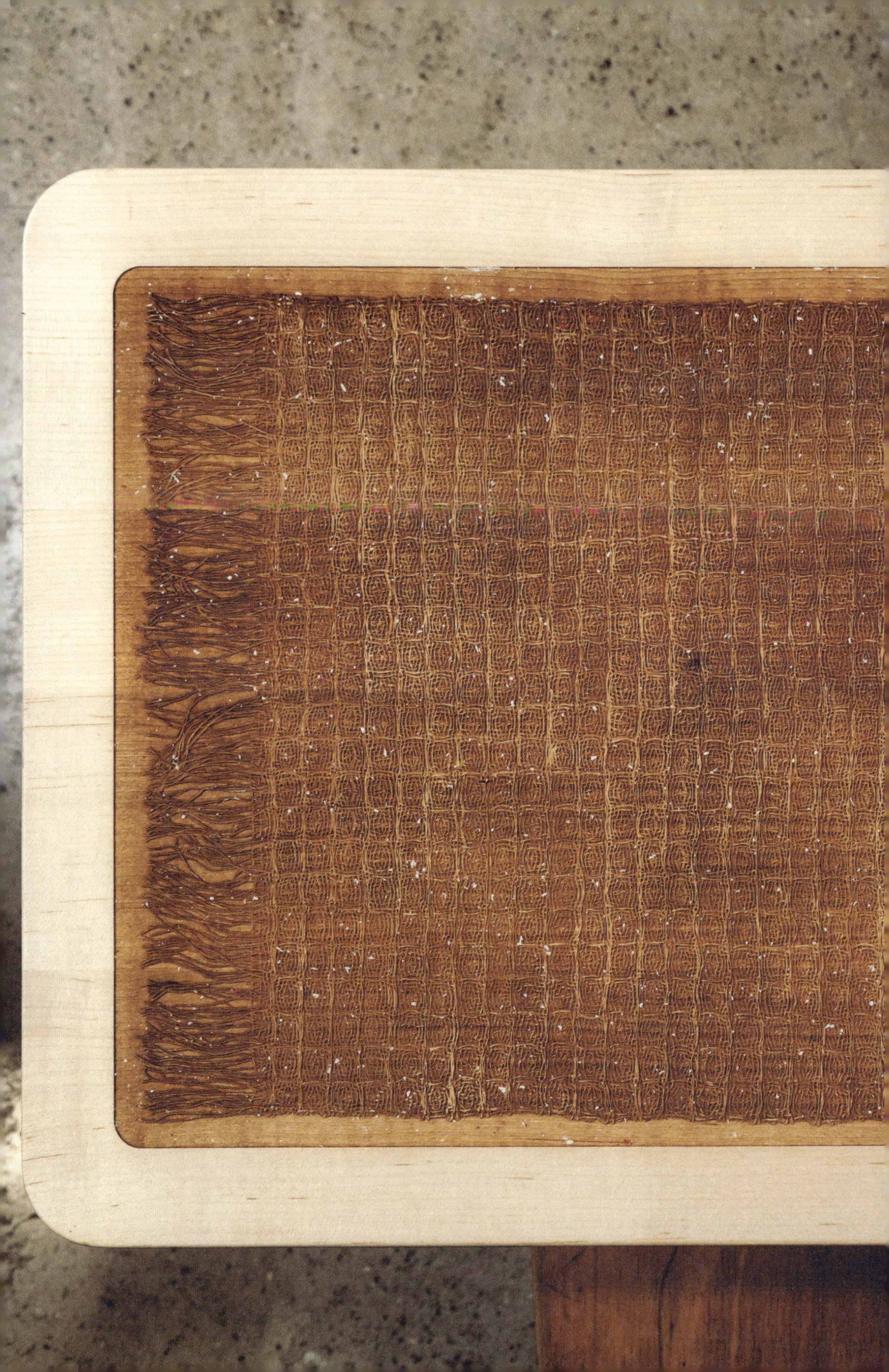

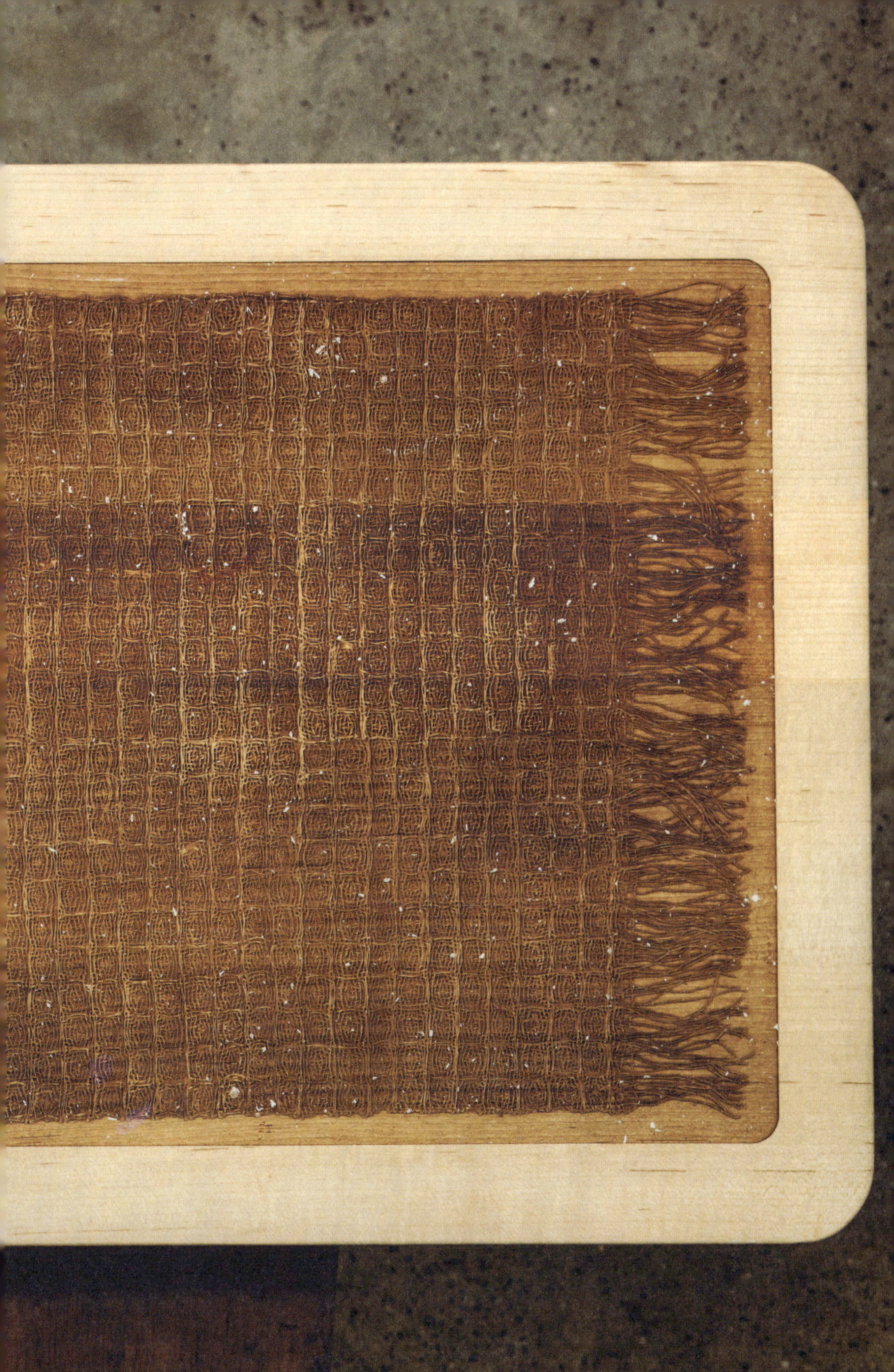

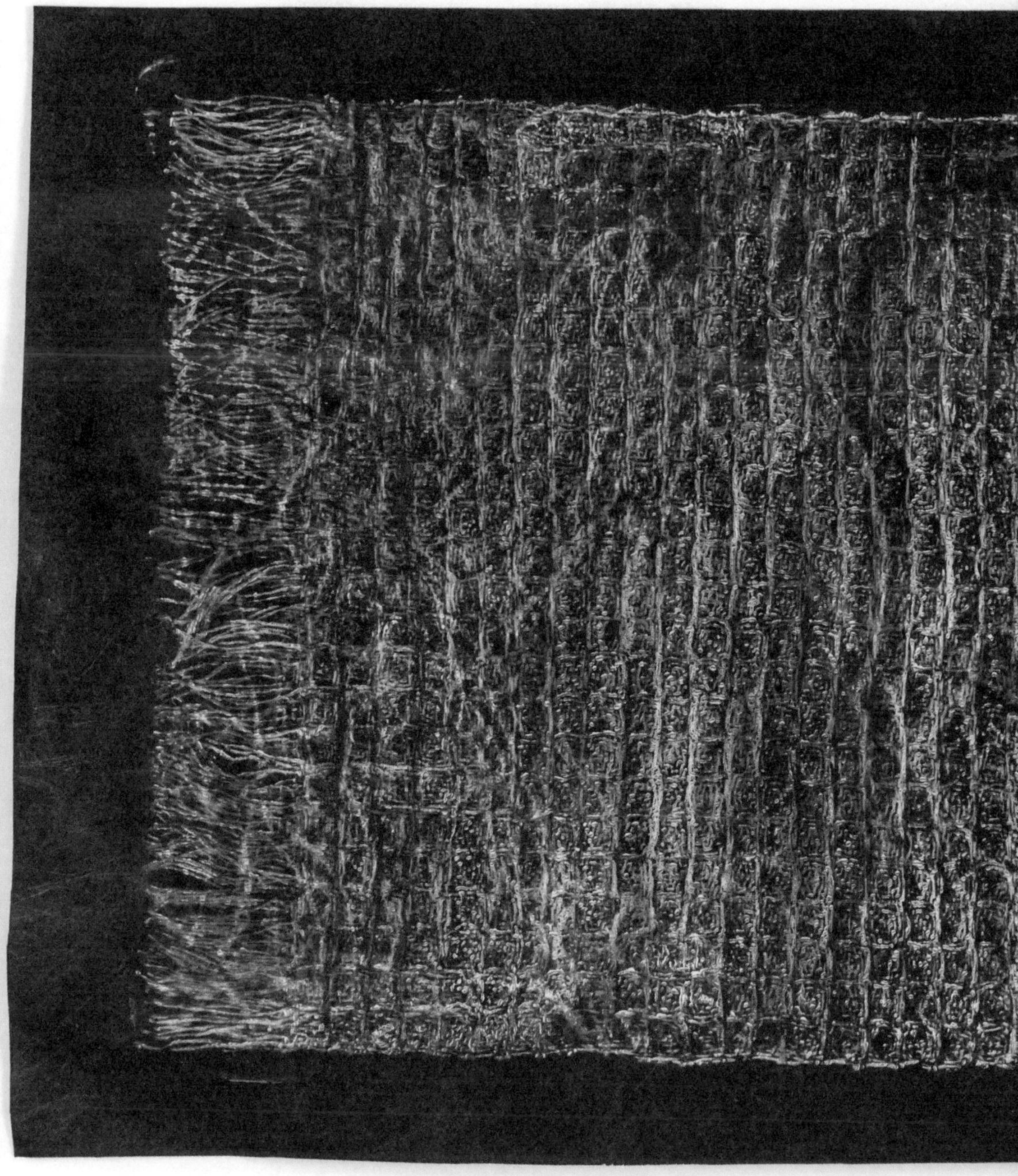

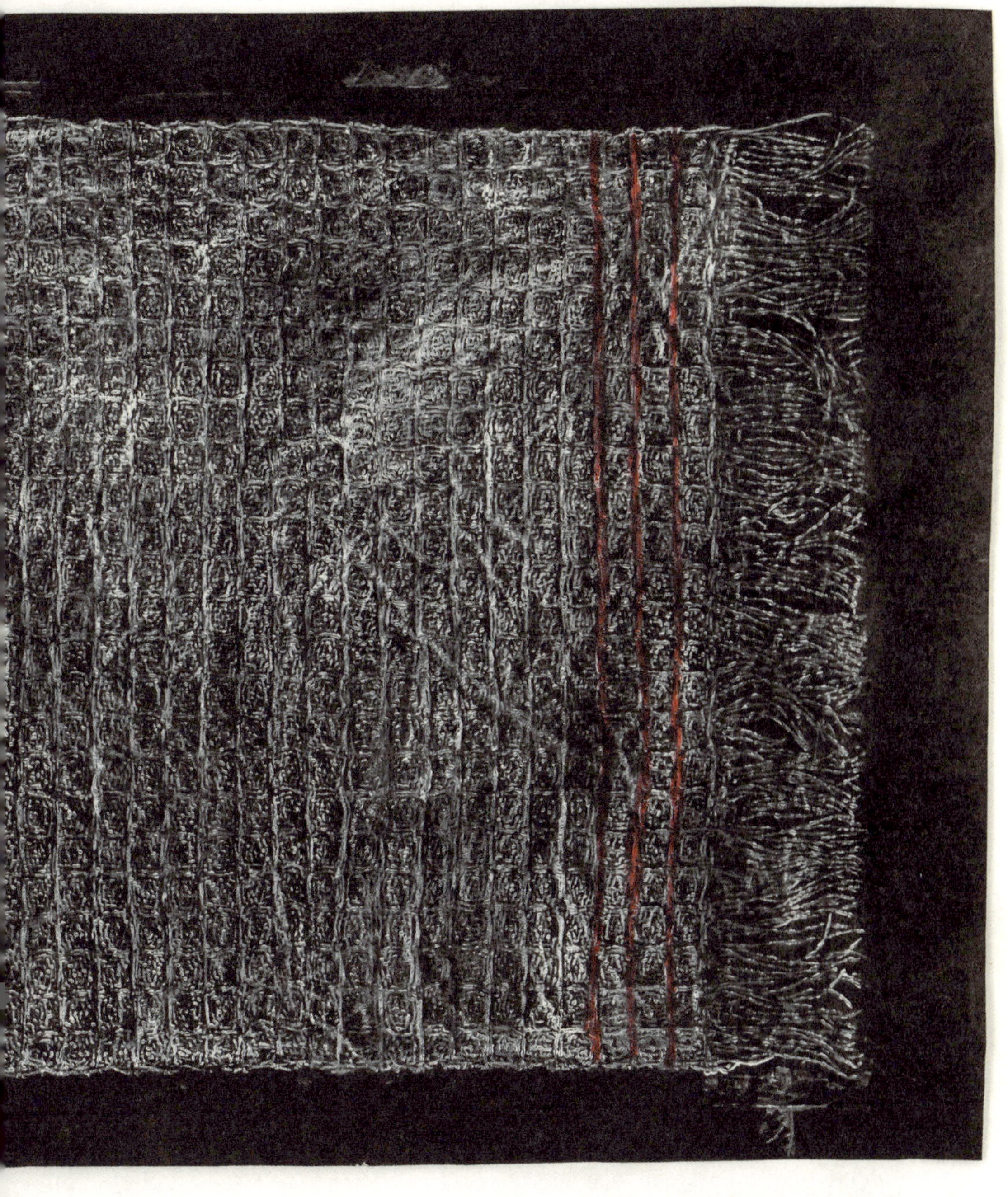

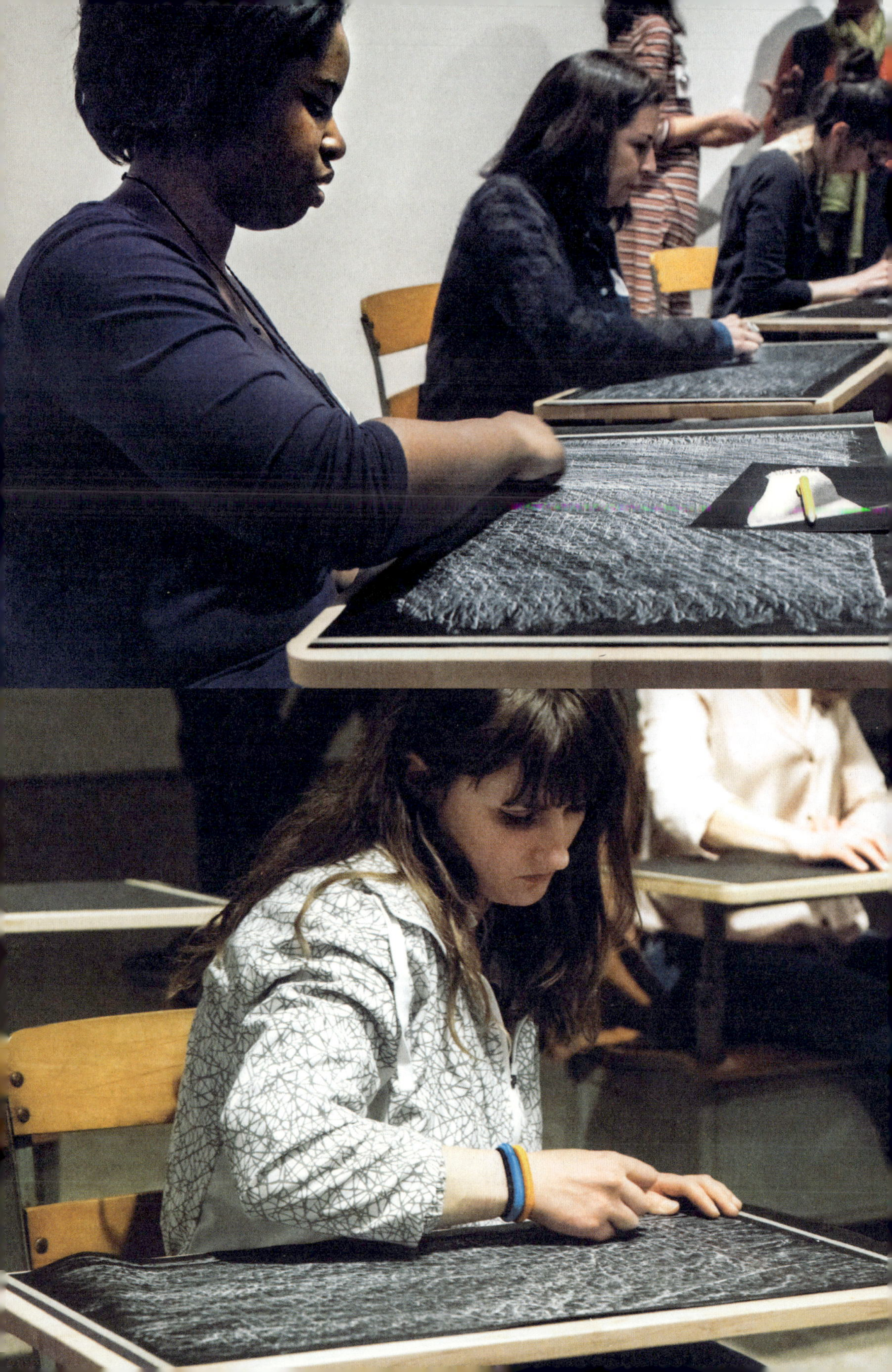

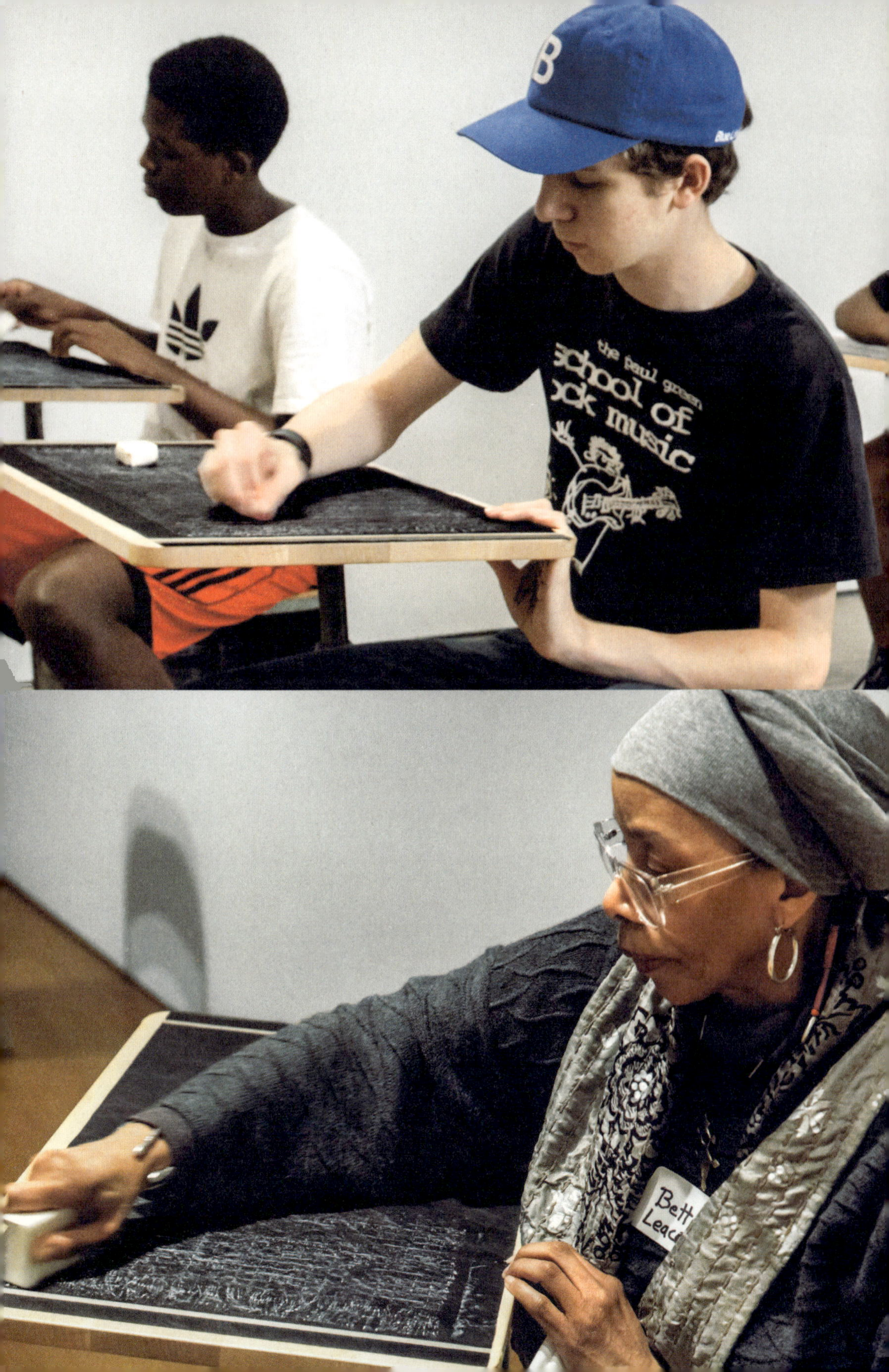
the paul green
school of
ock music

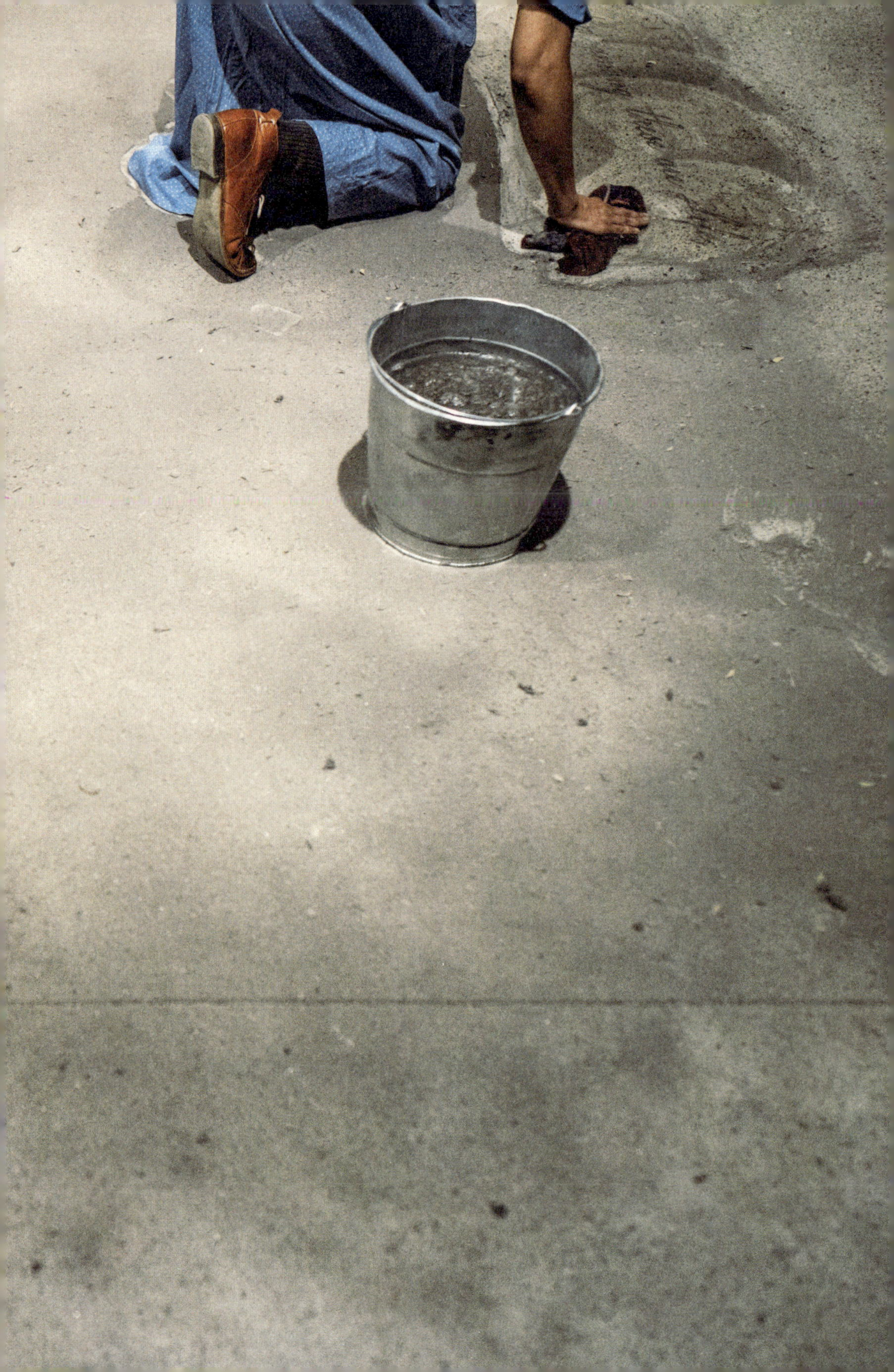

Reversals

In *Reversals*, Clark employs one of the commercially-produced items catalogued in *Propaganda* (2019, pp. 84, 86–89)—a dishcloth printed with the image of the Confederate Battle Flag—to wash a floor covered with dust gathered from Independence Hall and Declaration House in Philadelphia. Wearing a dress fashioned after the one worn by Ella Watson in *American Gothic, Washington, D.C.*, Gordon Parks' iconic 1942 photograph, the artist reveals a passage of text from the Preamble of the Declaration of Independence. As Clark cleans the concrete floor while crouched on one knee, the gesture of contemporary activists like Colin Kaepernick comes to mind. (Kaepernick is an NFL player who sparked a national debate about activism in professional sports by "taking a knee" on the field each time the national anthem was played at the beginning of a game to protest racial injustice.) *Reversals* presents us with an opportunity to re-examine these words and their history. It centers and honors the legacy of social justice work done by individuals, those in the shadows as well as the limelight, while acknowledging the legacy of racial injustice and the work that remains to achieve the ideals stated in this nation's founding documents, first among them "that all men are created equal."

Reversals, 2019. Reproduction of Ella Watson's dress from the photograph *American Gothic, Washington, D.C.* by Gordon Parks (1942), dust from Independence Hall and Declaration House, bucket, water, stenciled text, and towel commercially printed with the Confederate Battle Flag. In collaboration with The Fabric Workshop and Museum, Philadelphia

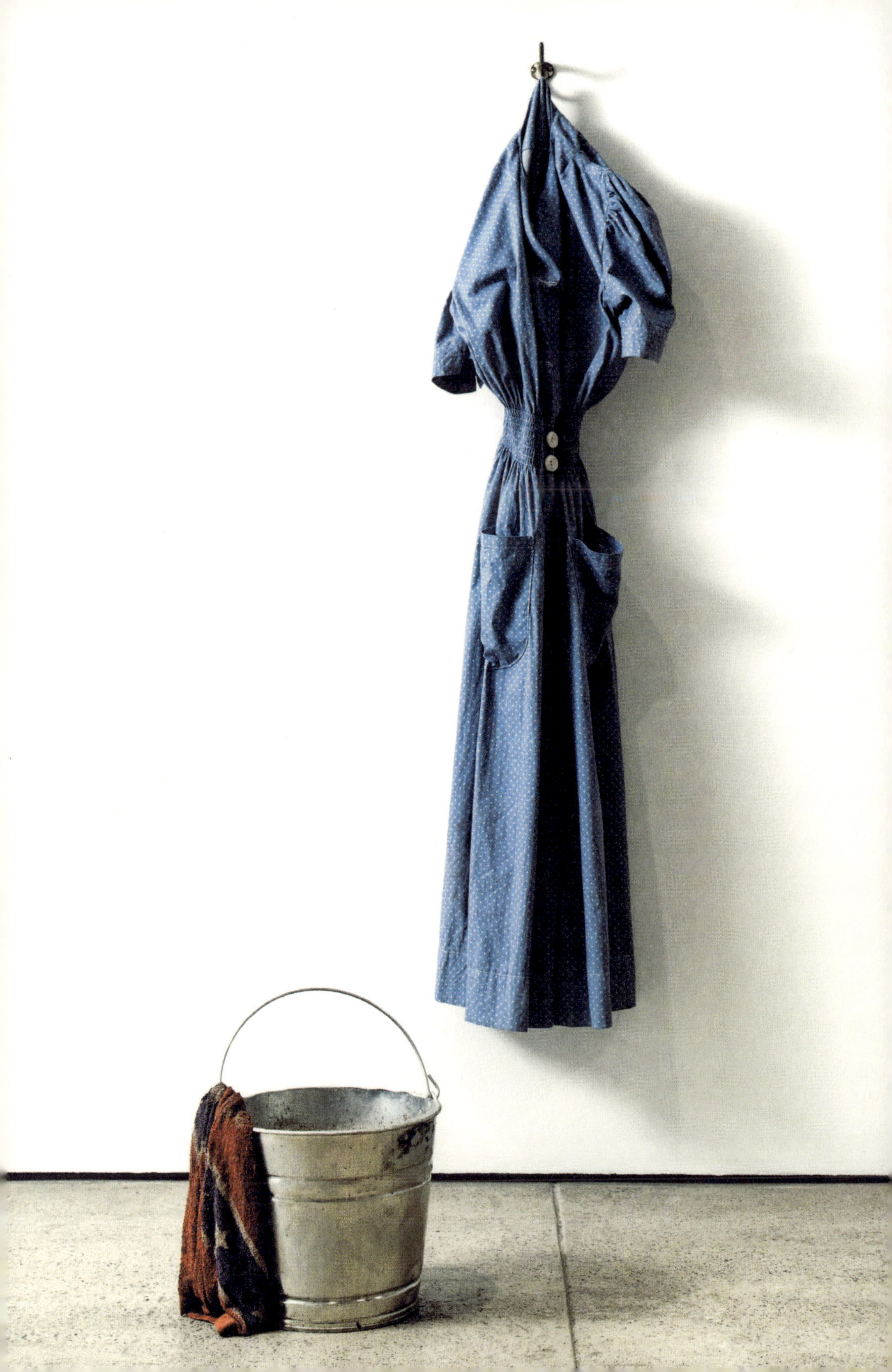

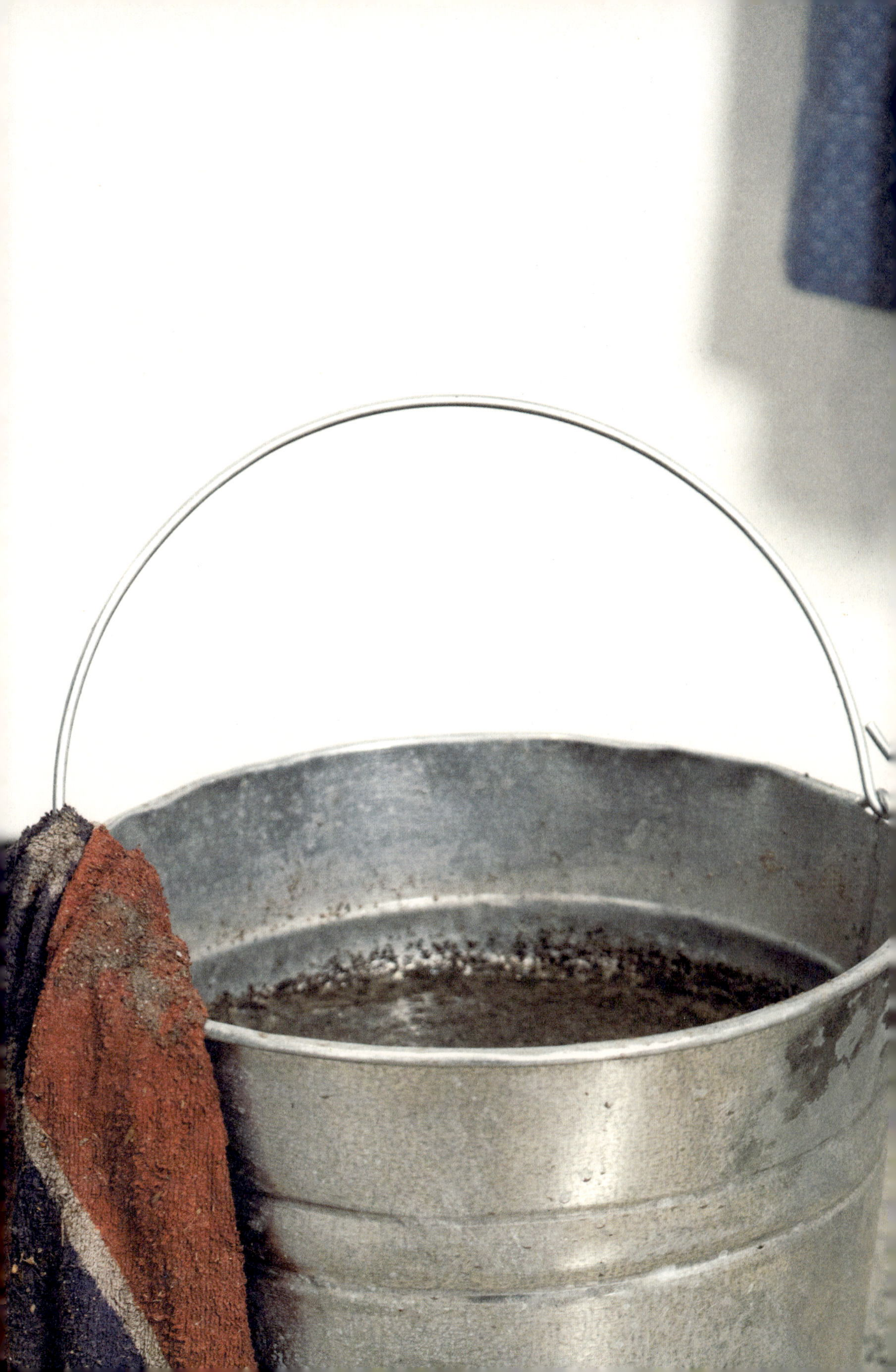

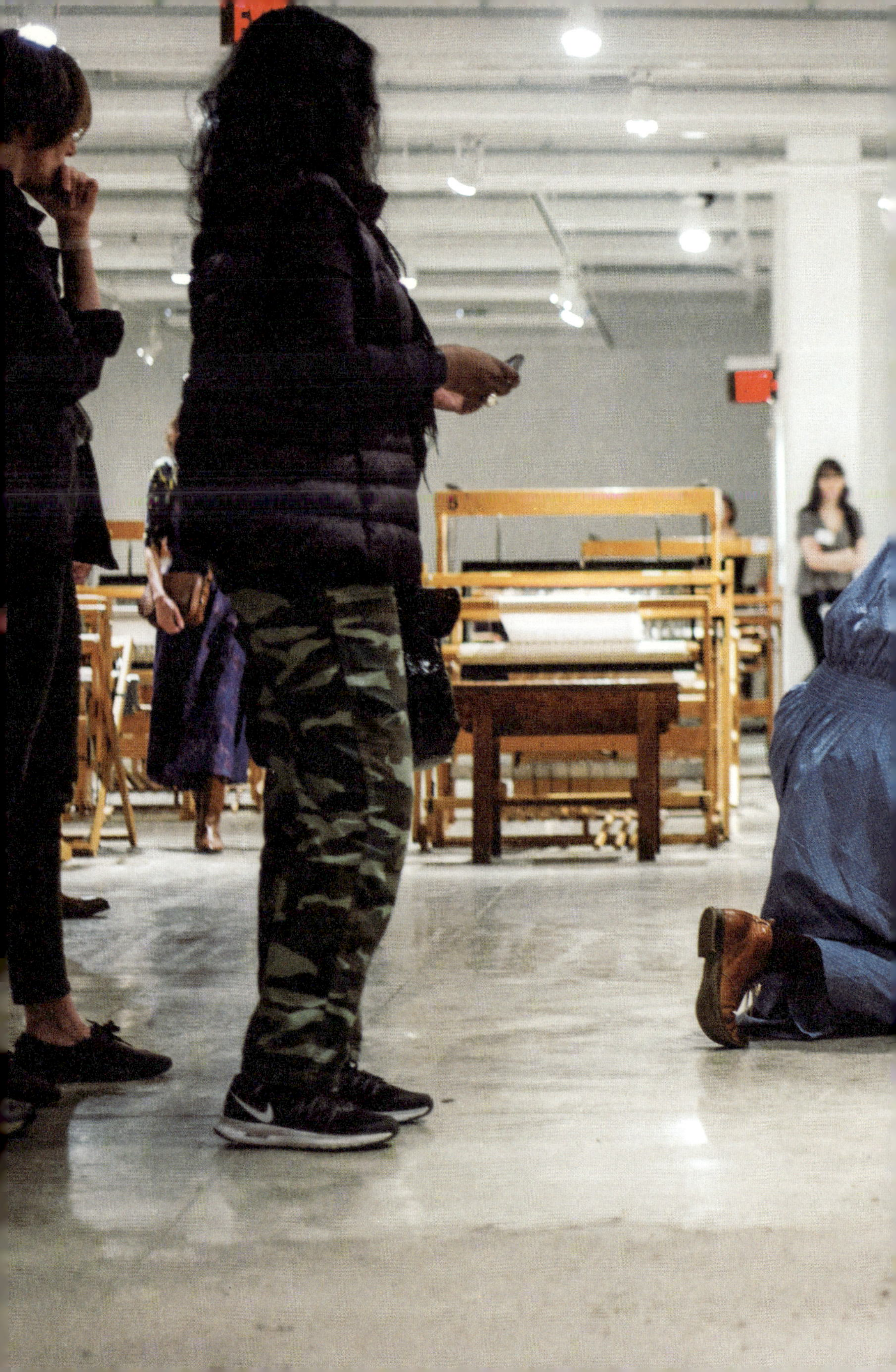

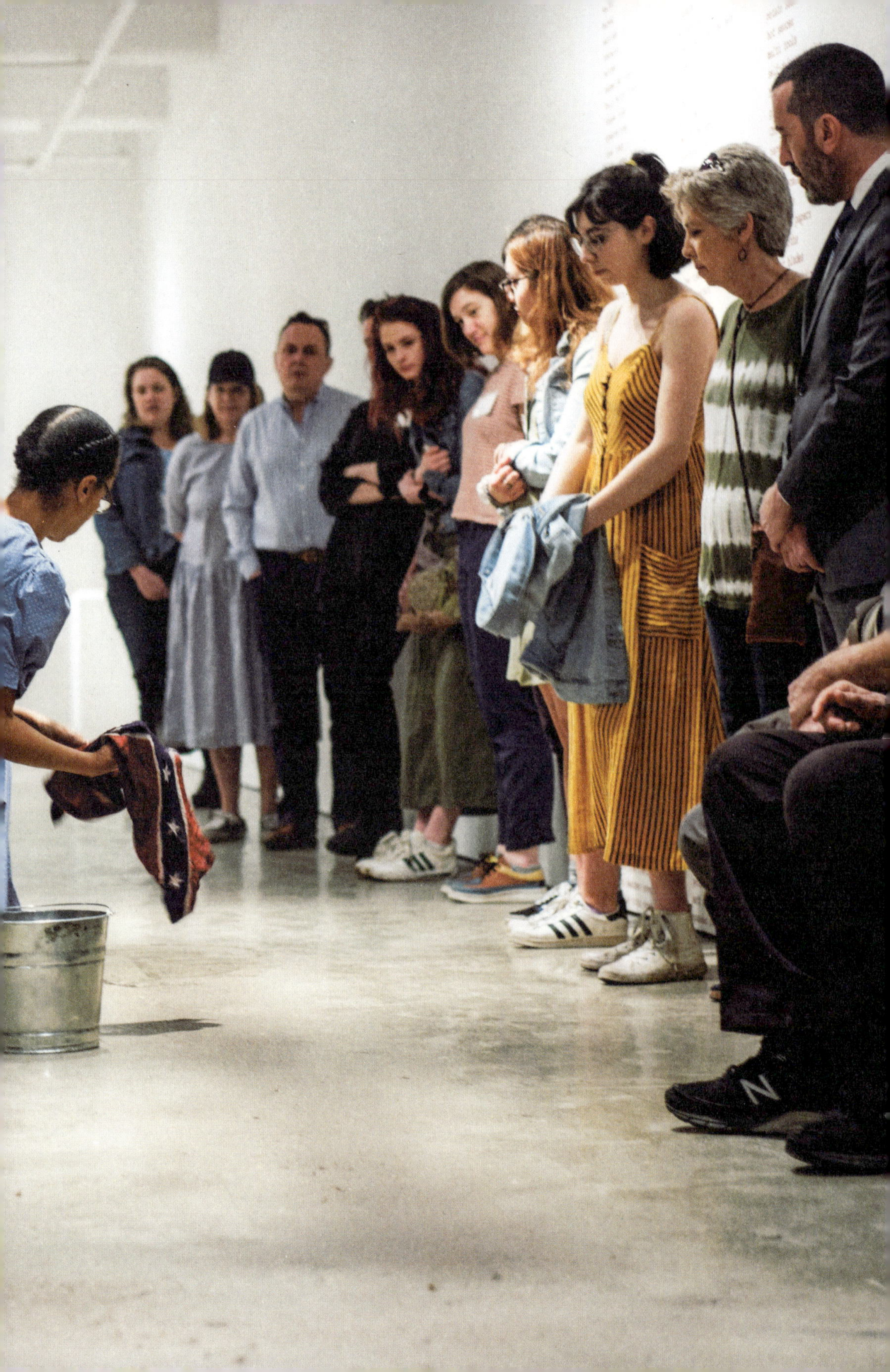

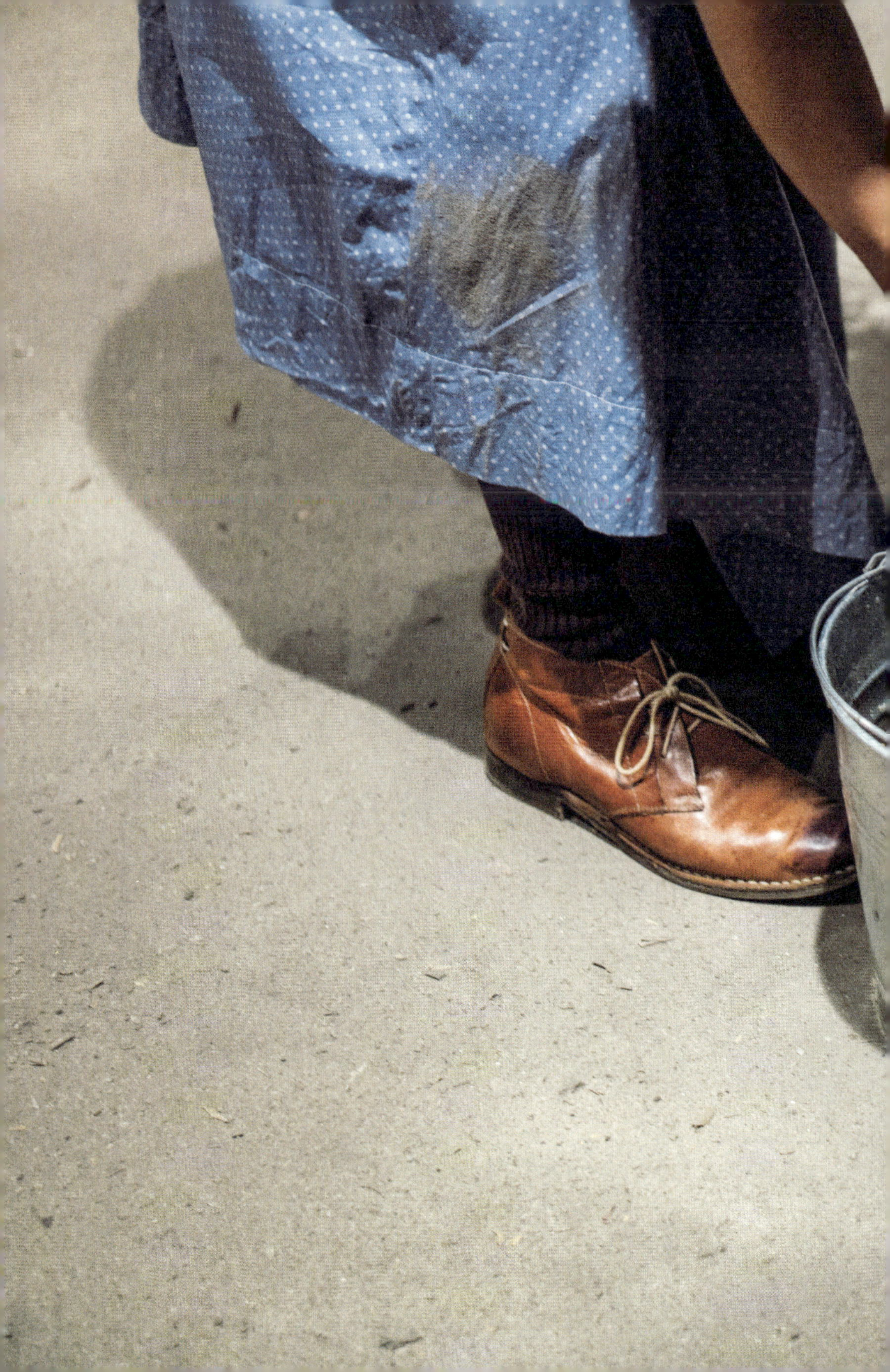

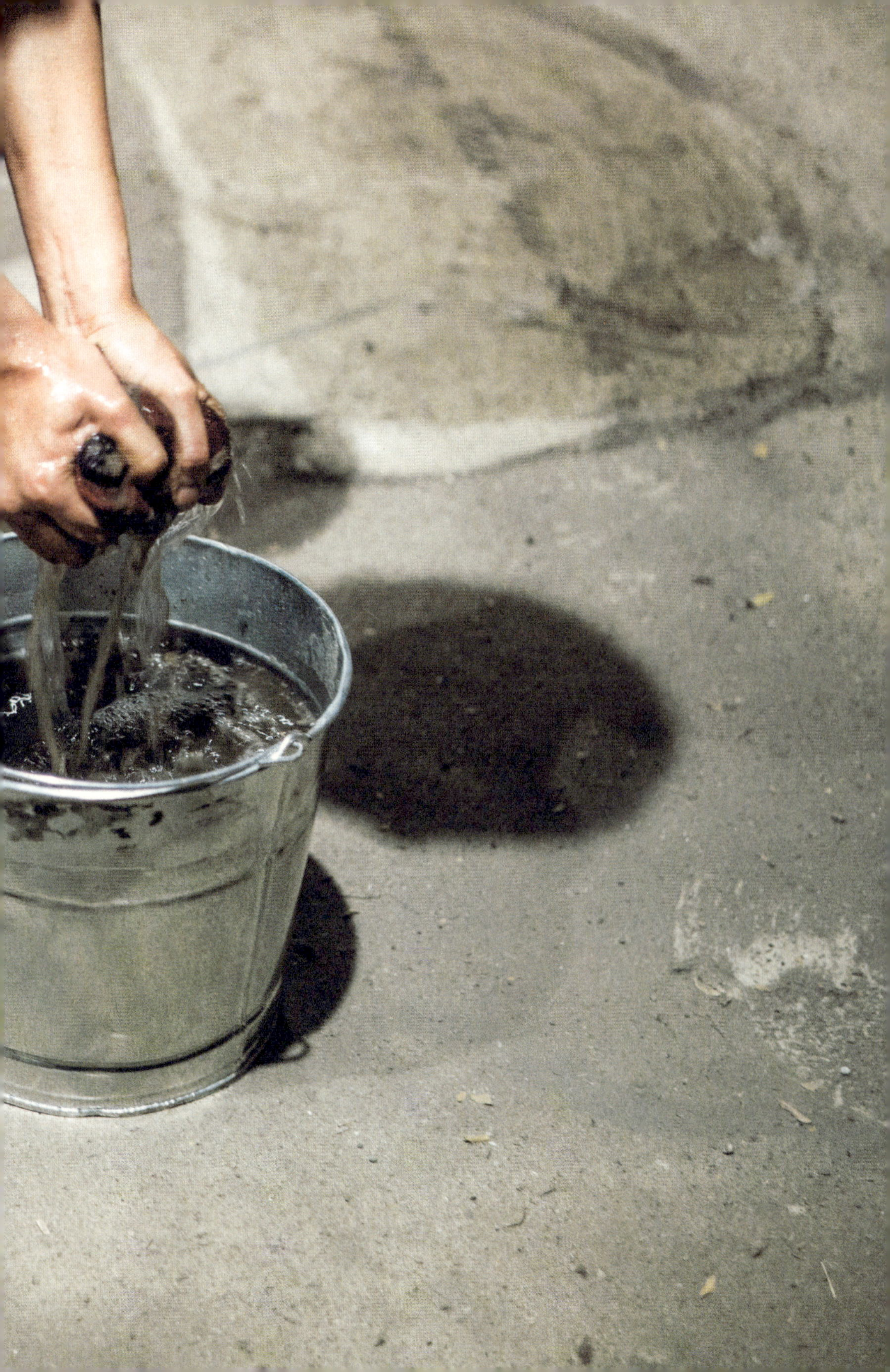

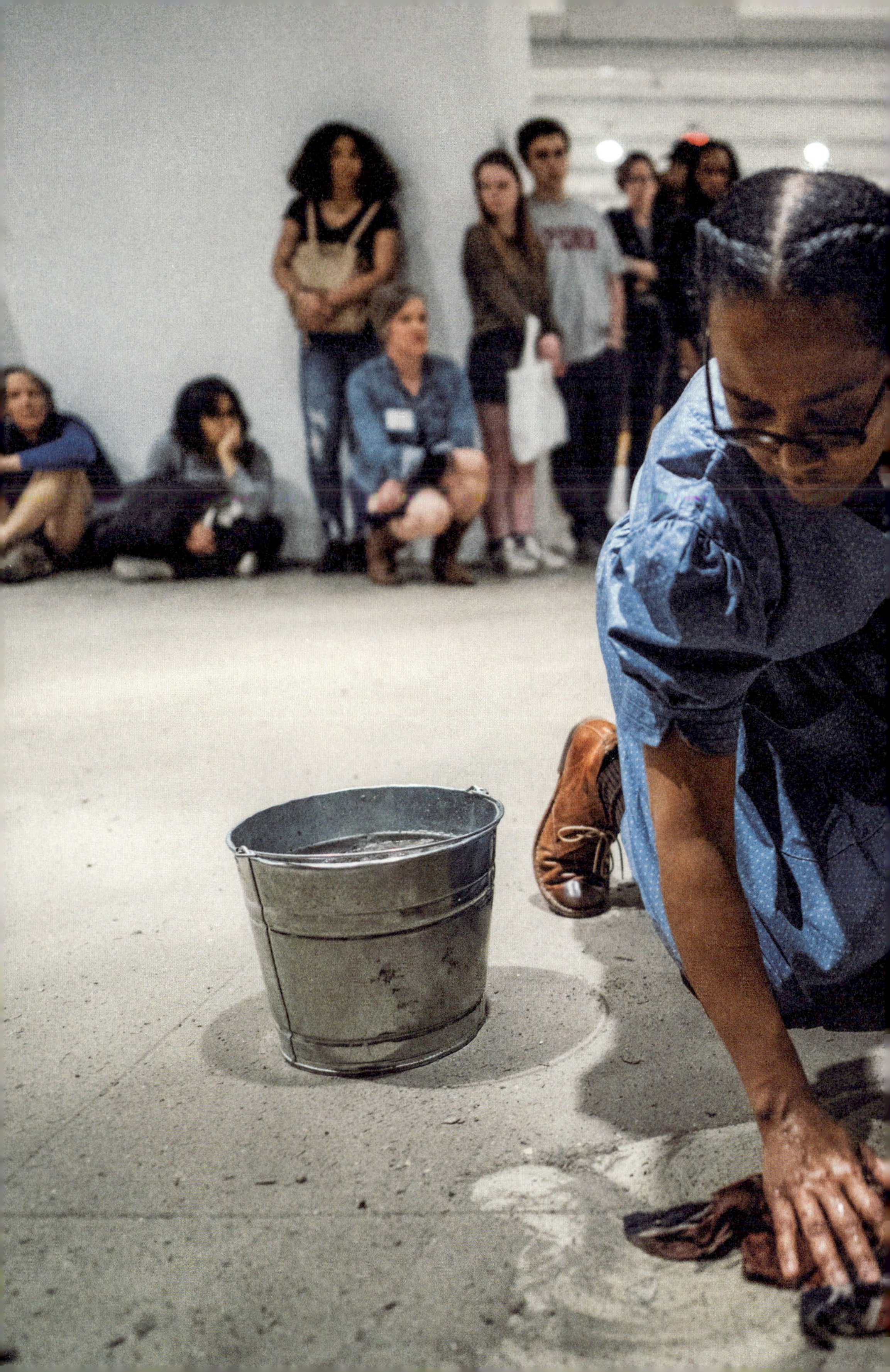

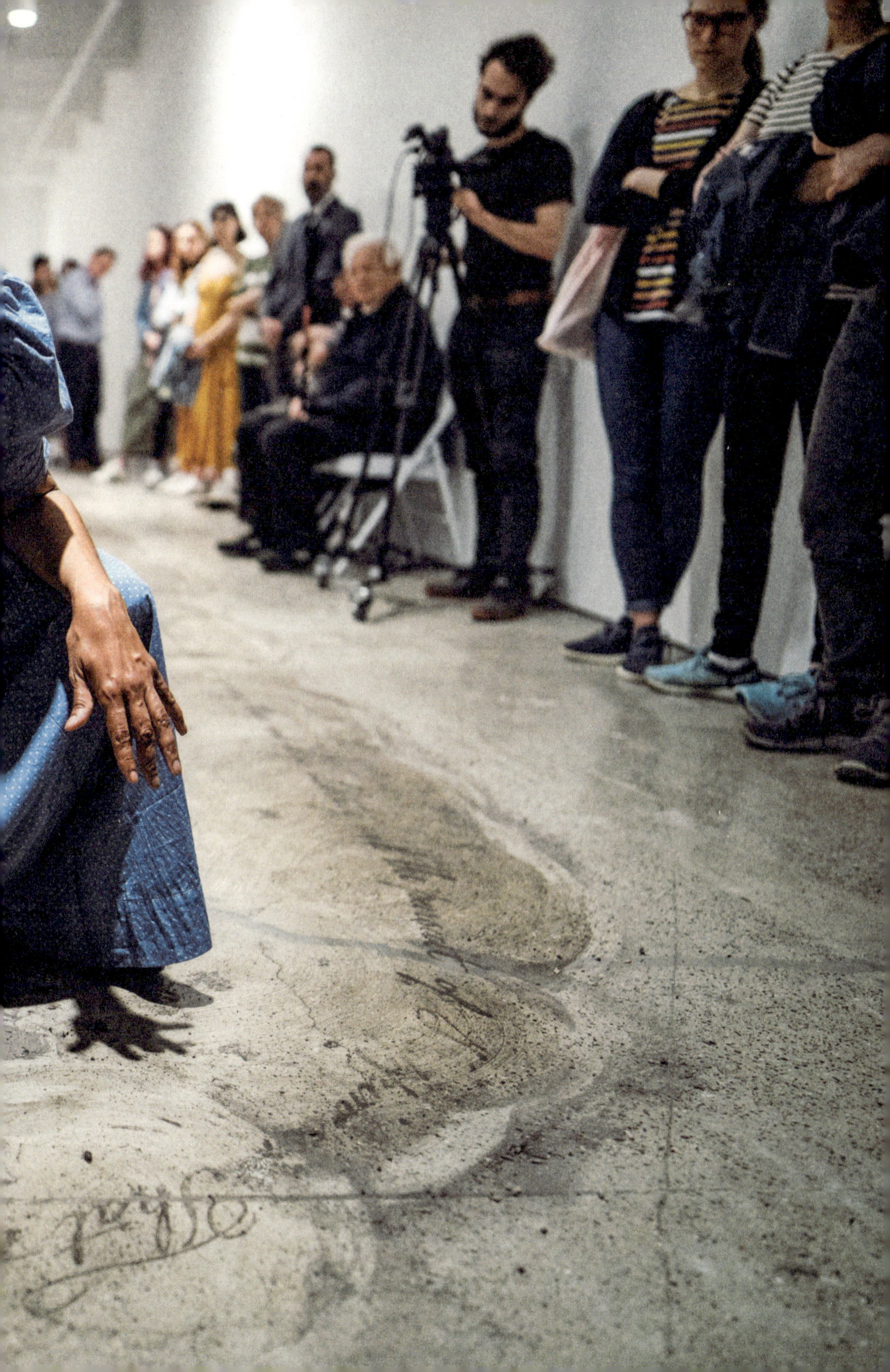

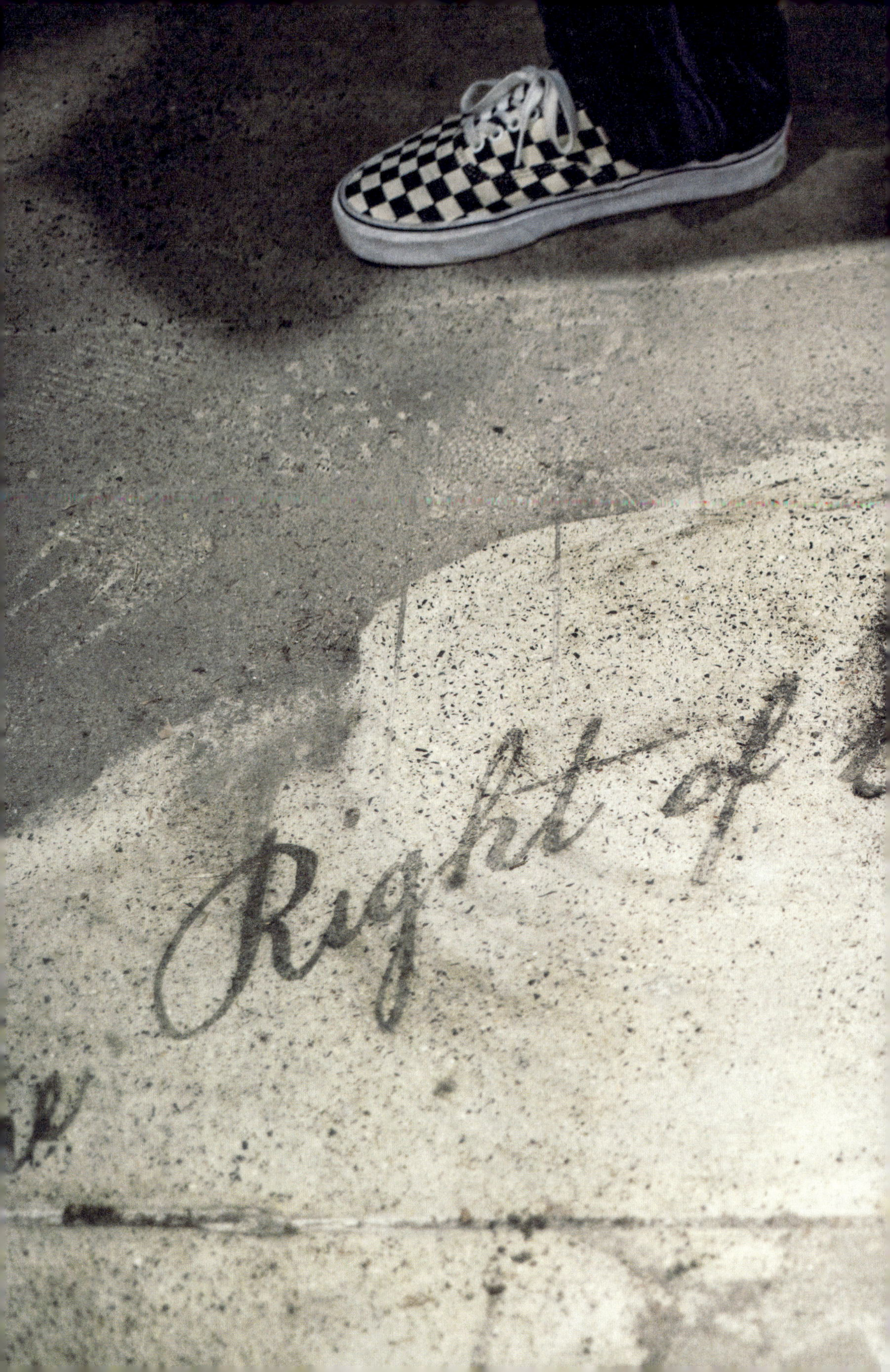

Right of

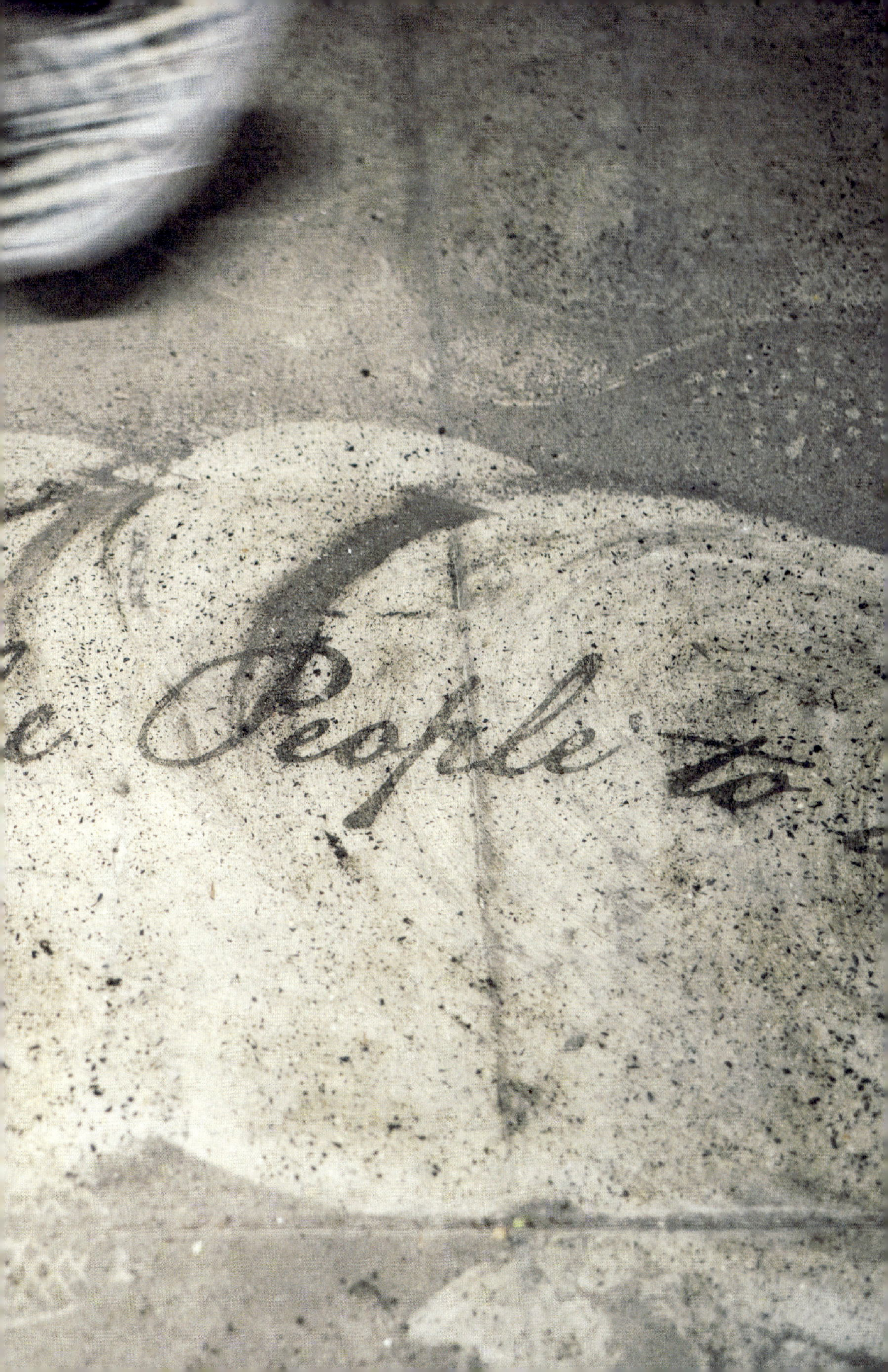
People's

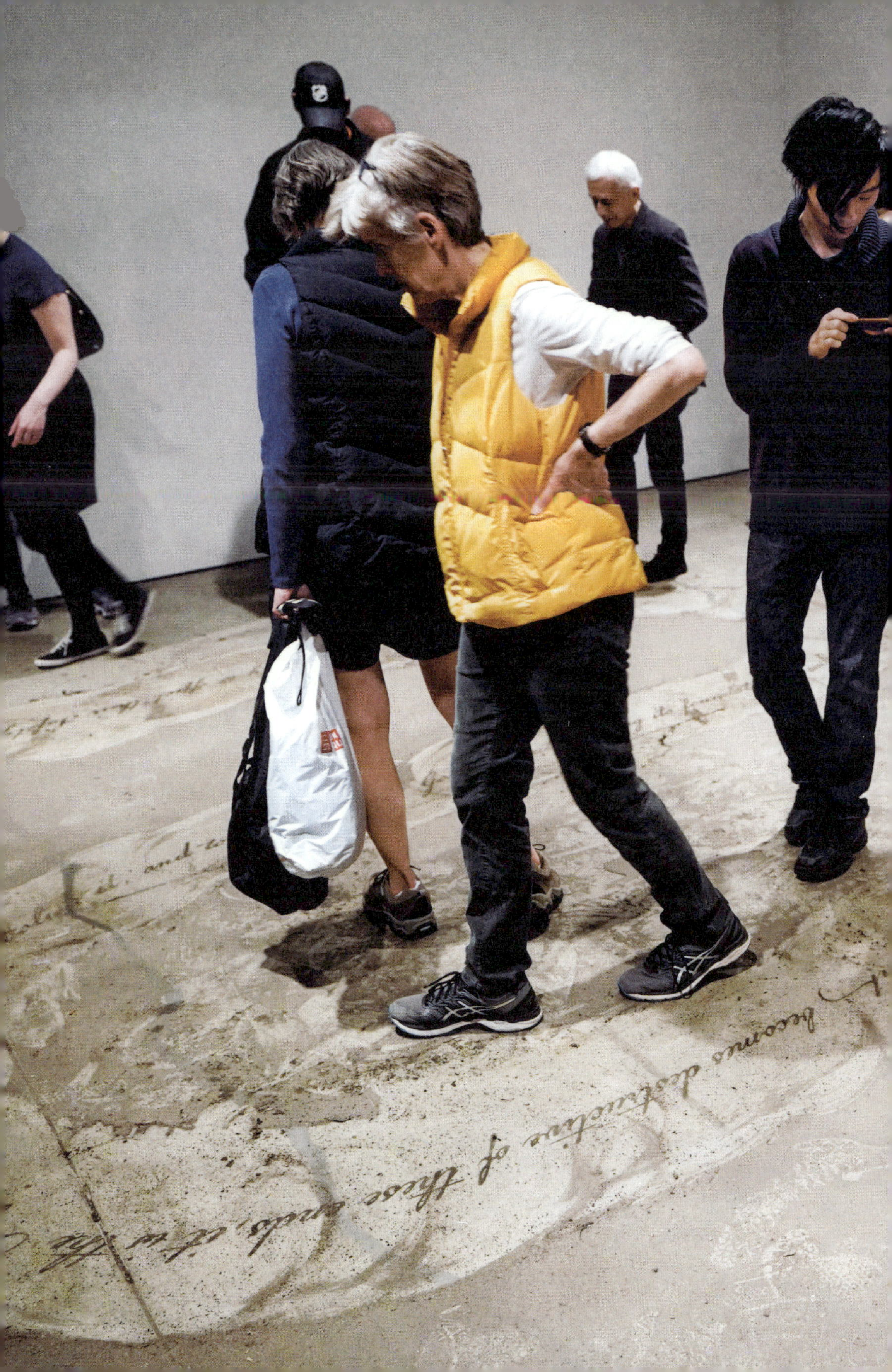

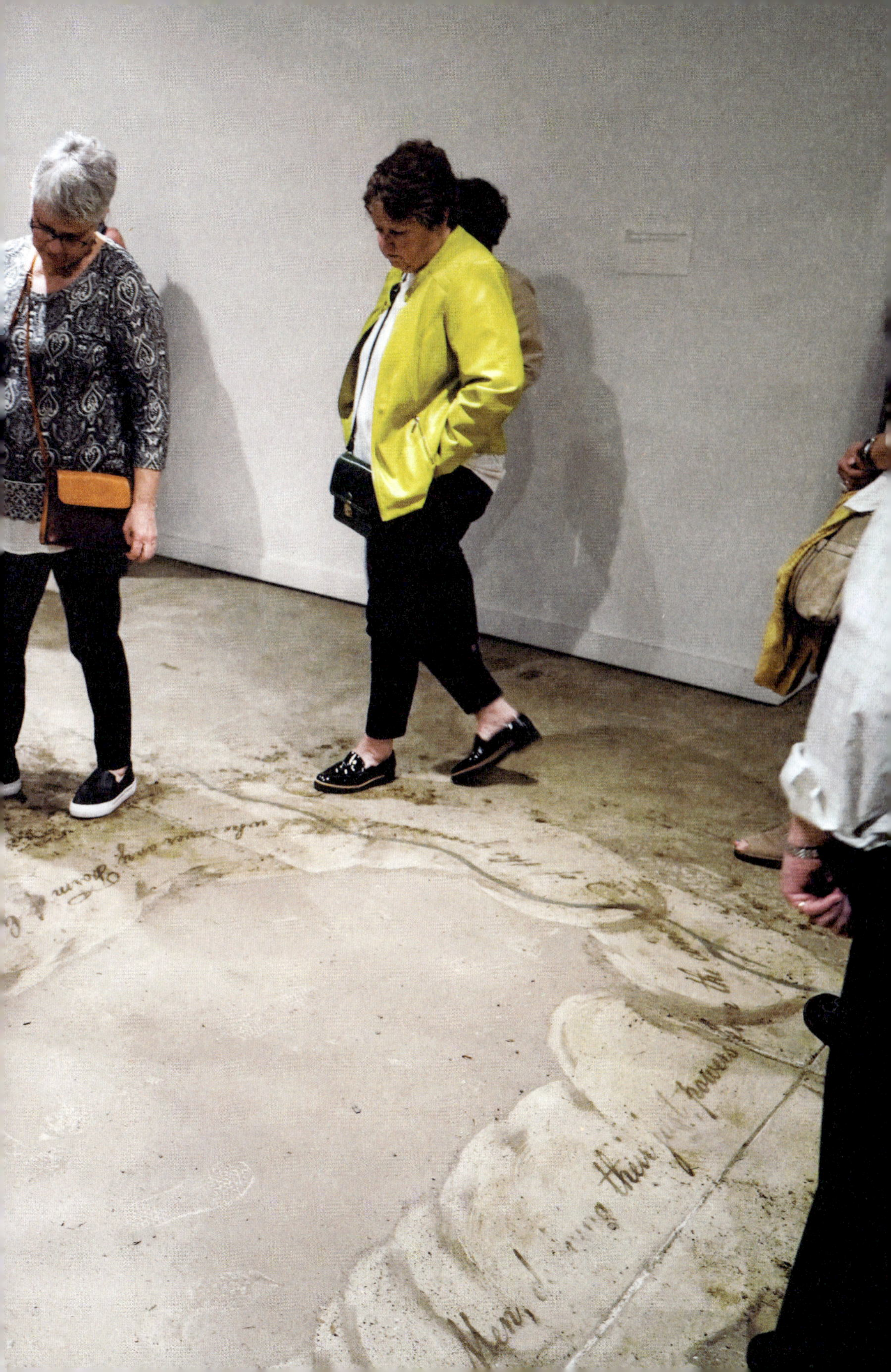

sneakers

wedding rings

umbrellas

headbands

cosmetics bags

dishcloths

drawstring bags

cowboy boots

coin purses

shoelaces

Propaganda

Although the Confederates used many different flags during the Civil War, one has become so well known that it is simply called the Confederate flag. Though its proper title is the Confederate Battle Flag, and it was specifically the flag of General Robert E. Lee's Army of Northern Virginia (not the official flag of the Confederate States), it now symbolizes the Confederate ideology for many Americans. Its insidious ubiquity permeates daily life and continues to play a divisive and contentious role in the United States. It is routinely slipped into popular culture, masquerading as a "benign" symbol of southern culture, as in its use in the late 1970s and early 1980s television show *Dukes of Hazzard*, while simultaneously being brandished as a symbol of white supremacy and white supremacist terrorism. *Propaganda* presents the myriad ways that the Battle Flag is commercially available and disseminated in present-day America. Though it comprises hundreds of items, this list is not comprehensive yet reveals the extent to which the flag has become propaganda. Imagine if the surrender rather than the battle was what we held in our collective memory. If the Truce Flag were memorialized as *the* symbol of the Civil War, might it have served as a compass for the work of reparations, reconciliation, and justice?

Title Wall

Further confirmation of the persistent and widespread use of Confederate motifs emerged when sourcing the color to paint the wall that would display the exhibition title. The perfect color to match the tiny red stripes in the Confederate Flag of Truce was produced by Benjamin Moore, color 2080-20: Confederate Red. This irony—the paint was purchased on the eve of the exhibition's opening—exemplifies the unabashed and seemingly unexamined romanticization of the Confederacy. The company has since rebranded the color as Patriot Red.

Left, pages 86–89: *Propaganda*, 2019. Vinyl. Dimensions variable. In collaboration with The Fabric Workshop and Museum, Philadelphia

Page 91: *Title Wall*, 2019. Benjamin Moore wall paint. Dimensions variable. In collaboration with The Fabric Workshop and Museum, Philadelphia

backpacks
duffle bags
dog tags
high-top sneakers
wedding rings
umbrellas
headbands
cosmetics bags
dishcloths
drawstring bags
cowboy boots
coin purses
shoelaces
lanyards
keychains
sweatshirts
t-shirts
sleeveless button-up shirts
tank tops
tube tops
muscle shirts
men's briefs
bikinis
one-piece swimsuits
men's swim trunks
women's tank tops
vests
dresses
women's booty shorts
lingerie
leggings
panties
thongs
bras
denim jackets
men's dress shirts
sarongs
hooded blankets
tube tops
window mounted car flags
rearview mirror hanging dice
spandex auto hood covers
valve stem covers
auto headrest covers
trailer hitch covers

coaster
ashtray
coin di
beverag
pint gl
suncatc
bottle
tea tow
thermom
shot gl
coffee
travel
tumbler
mouse p
flasks
salt an
mailbox
trinket
toilet
bath to
curtain
valance
light s
wall ou
windchi
clocks
area ru
tapestr
lamps
welcome
photo f
table r
placema
water b
garden
music b
wooden
door ta
cutting
decorat
candle
pencil
bath ma
spandex

es

r shakers

late covers
vers

ow pillows

covers

gift bags
Christmas stockings
paper plates
yo-yos
nail decals
hard hats
wrapping papers
washcloths
razor blades
tactical folding knives
skull decorations
gun grips
glass handpipes
ropes
gun holsters
clip art
spitoons
jigsaw puzzles
piggy banks
action figures
nipple pasties
pet collars
dog leashes
dog bandanas
ski masks
beach towels
playing cards
beach bags
skateboards
golf balls
guitar picks
coolers
hockey masks
gloves
folding camp chairs
horse saddles
horse reins
guitars
guitar straps
cornhole sets
yoga mats
banjo straps
water shoes
and more...

skullcaps, baseball caps, cowboy hats, beanies, visor
purses, silicon wristbands, money clips, necklaces, c
sunglasses, sunglasses straps, tote bags, checkbook
watches, belt buckles, belts, wallets, purses, earring
tongue rings, eyebrow rings, nose rings, nipple rings,
rings, umbrellas, headbands, cosmetics bags, dishclo
lanyards, keychains, sweatshirts, t-shirts, sleevele
men's briefs, bikinis, one-piece swimsuits, men's sw
shorts, lingerie, leggings, panties, thongs, bras, de
tube tops, window-mounted car flags, rearview mirror
auto headrest covers, trailer hitch covers, travel n
floor mats, antenna balls, truck rear-window graphi
helmets, motorcycle flag mounts, license plate frames,
knobs, seat covers , baby blankets, baby onesies, you
baby car seat covers, toy soldier sets, toy cars, flag
magnets, bumper stickers, stickers, license plates, m
flight wings, posters, blankets, bedsheet sets, three-
pot holders, decorative signs, coasters, ashtrays,
bottle openers, tea towels, thermometers, shot glass
salt and pepper shakers, mailbox covers, trinket bo
switch plate covers, wall outlet covers, windchimes,
frames, table runners, placemats, water bottles, ga
boards, decorative throw pillows, candle holders, per
calendars, night-lights, coffee tables, vinyl wall d
throwing knives, air fresheners, plastic cups, wind
cases, cell phone cases, cell phone grips, compact
craft ribbons, temporary tattoos, party streamer flag
pens, postcards, commemorative coins, greeting card
sauces, multi tools, self-defense toggles, hand fans,
decals, hard hats, wrapping papers, washcloths, razo
grips, glass handpipes, ropes, gun holsters, clip a
nipple pasties, pet collars, dog leashes, dog banda
skateboards, golf balls, guitar picks, coolers, ho
horse reins, guitars, guitar straps, cornhole sets,

cket hats, fedoras, scarves, bandanas, concealed carry
unds, socks, neckties, bow ties, cufflinks, suspenders,
s, carabiners, flip-flops, scrunchies, do-rags, pocket
acelets, watches, gauged ear plugs, belly button rings,
packs, duffle bags, dog tags, high-top sneakers, wedding
drawstring bags, cowboy boots, coin purses, shoelaces,
tton-up shirts, tank tops, tube tops, muscle shirts,
nks, women's tank tops, vests, dresses, women's booty
ackets, men's dress shirts, sarongs, hooded blankets,
ng dice, spandex auto hood covers, valve stem covers,
illows, spare tire covers, steering wheel covers, car
otorcycle bells, motorcycle cup holders, motorcycle
se plate frame fastener bolts, auto interior door lock
shirts, baby t-shirts, toddler t-shirts, diaper bags,
x 6 inches to 10 x 15 feet, refrigerator magnets, car
ycle license plates, lapel pins, embroidered patches,
comforter sets, shower curtains, aprons, oven mitts,
dishes, beverage coozies, pint glasses, suncatchers,
offee mugs, travel mugs, tumblers, mouse pads, flasks,
toilet seats, bath towels, curtains, valances, light
ks, area rugs, tapestries, lamps, welcome mats, photo
flags, music boxes, wooden boxes, door tags, cutting
olders, bath mats, spandex door covers, paperweights,
, ceiling fan pulls, statues, pocket knives, knives,
snuff cases, cigarette cases, knife cases, lighter
rs, Santa hats, Christmas ornaments, fidget spinners,
lloons, dream catchers, toothpicks, writing journals,
ncils, seasoning mixes, lighters, potato sacks, hot
bags, Christmas stockings, paper plates, yo-yos, nail
des, tactical folding knives, skull decorations, gun
pitoons, jigsaw puzzles, piggy banks, action figures,
ski masks, beach towels, playing cards, beach bags,
masks, gloves, folding camp chairs, horse saddles,
mats, banjo straps, water shoes, , , and more . . .

cherry wine
2080-30
confederate red
2080-20
raspberry truffle
2080-10
BENJAMIN MOORE®
COLOR PREVIEW® 2080

Benjamin Moore Paint Color 2080-20: Confederate Red

About the Artist

Sonya Clark is an artist and educator who draws from the legacy of crafted objects to tackle issues of nationhood, social injustice, and racial constructs. She is a professor of art at Amherst College in Massachusetts. From 2006 to 2017, she served as chair of the Craft and Material Studies Department at Virginia Commonwealth University and received the university's highest award, the Commonwealth Professorship. Formerly she was Baldwin-Bascom Professor of Creative Arts at the University of Wisconsin-Madison. She holds an MFA from Cranbrook Academy of Art. She also holds a BFA from the School of the Art Institute of Chicago. In 2015 she was awarded an honorary doctorate from her alma mater, Amherst College, where she received a BA.

Clark has exhibited in over 350 museums and galleries in Europe, Africa, Asia, Australia, and the Americas. Her work is in the permanent collections of the Museum of Fine Arts Boston, Philadelphia Museum of Art, National Museum of Women in the Arts in Washington, D.C., Indianapolis Museum of Art, and the Virginia Museum of Fine Arts in Richmond, among others. She is the recipient of a number of awards, including those from Art Matters, United States Artists, Pollock-Krasner Foundation, Art Prize, and Anonymous Was a Woman. She has also been selected for residencies at Red Gate in Beijing; BAU Camargo in Cassis, France; Rockefeller Bellagio in Bellagio, Italy; Smithsonian Artist Research Fellowship in Washington, D.C.; Civitella Ranieri in Umbertide, Italy; Yaddo in Saratoga Springs, New York; and an Affiliate Fellowship at the American Academy in Rome. Her work has been reviewed in the *New York Times, Philadelphia Inquirer, Sculpture, Artforum, Los Angeles Times, Hyperallergic, Mother Jones*, and *Huffington Post*. Deeply committed to the field of craft, Clark has also served on the boards of the American Craft Council in Minneapolis, Textile Museum at George Washington University in Washington, D.C., and Haystack Mountain School of Crafts in Deer Isle, Maine.

Acknowledgments

The artist is deeply grateful to the people at the many institutions who were instrumental to the realization of this exhibition, to the individuals and organizations who contributed to this catalogue, to the engaged audience, to the Smithsonian Artist Research Fellowship, and to all those who continue to fight for equality and justice.

Funders

The Andy Warhol Foundation for
  The Visual Arts
Amherst College
Agnes Gund
National Endowment for the Arts
Goya Contemporary Gallery &
  Goya-Girl Press
Sara and Bill Morgan
Rotasa Fund
John Meyerhoff, M.D. and Lenel
  Srochi-Meyerhoff
Judith S. Weisman

Program Collaborators

*The African American Museum in
  Philadelphia*
James Claiborne, Public Programming
  Manager
Dejay Duckett, Director of Curatorial
  Services
Hannah Wallace, Educational
  Programming Manager

Family Heir-Loom Weavers, Inc.

Weavers and Weaving Instructors

Alyssa Zeboritz
Susannah Dotson
Kelly Kuykendall
Allen West
Nami Yamamoto
Isabella Amstrup
Enrica Ferrero
Becky Flax
Francesca Schnalke
Ben Jones
Kristen Tynan
Victoria Tertychny
Donna Madeline Tavernier

Graphic Design

Matsumoto Incorporated
Takaaki Matsumoto
Amy Wilkins
Robin Brunelle

FWM Studio Team

Nami Yamamoto
Avery Lawrence
Allen West
Zack Ingram
Kelly Kuykendall
Abby Lutz

Interns

Emily Dombrovskaya
Amaya Bullock

About The Fabric Workshop and Museum

The Fabric Workshop and Museum was founded in 1977 with a visionary purpose: to stimulate experimentation among contemporary artists and to share the process of creating works of art with the public. Providing studio facilities, equipment, and expert technicians, FWM originally invited artists to experiment with fabric and later with a wide range of innovative materials and media. From the outset, FWM has also served as an education center for Philadelphia's youth who, as printing apprentices, learn technical and vocational skills along with approaches to creative expression.

Today, FWM is an internationally acclaimed contemporary art museum devoted to creating work with textiles and new media in collaboration with artists from such diverse backgrounds as sculpture, installation, video, painting, ceramics, and architecture. Research, construction, and fabrication occur on-site in studios that are open to the public, providing visitors an opportunity to see art being made from conception to completion. Ambitious exhibitions, publications, and wide-ranging educational programming enhance FWM's commitment to telling a story of contemporary art that highlights process along with product. FWM's collection includes not only complete works of art but also material research, samples, and prototypes, as well as photography and video of artists making and speaking about their work. FWM brings artistic investigation and discovery to the public, area schoolchildren in particular, to ensure and broaden their exposure to art and to advance the role of art as a catalyst for innovation and social connection. FWM offers an unparalleled experience to the most significant artists of our time, to students, and to the general public.

Marion Boulton Stroud (1939–2015),
*Founder and Artistic Director
(1977–2015)*

Susan Lubowsky Talbott, *Executive
Director*

Board of Directors
Officers
Maja Paumgarten Parker, *President*
Jill Bonovitz, *Vice President*
Eugene Mopsik, *Treasurer*
Lynn Hitschler, *Secretary*

Board Members
Jason Briggs
Sarah Jackson
Timothy Kearney
Emanuel Kelly
Ann T. Loftus, Esq.
Mary MacGregor Mather
Laurie McGahey
Margaret "Maggie" A. McGreal
John Ravenal
Joseph J. Rishel
Georgina Sanger
Katherine Sokolnikoff
David F. Stephens
Cynthia Stroud

Theodore R. Aronson, *Emeritus*
Richard P. Jaffe, Esq., *Emeritus*
Anne F. Wetzel, *Emeritus*
Samuel H. Young, *Emeritus*

Artist Advisory Committee
John Ravenal, *Chair*
Ian Berry
Francesco Bonami
Dan Byers
Valerie Cassel Oliver
Mel Chin
Paolo Colombo
Kathie DeShaw
Matthew Drutt
Russell Ferguson
Jennifer Gross
Paul Ha
Ann Hamilton
David Allen Hanks
Jun Kaneko
Tina Kukielski
Rick Lowe
Lisa Phillips
Mark Rosenthal
Paul Schimmel
Bennett Simpson
Patterson Sims
Robert Storr
Olga Viso
Yoshiko Wada
Kara Walker

as of December 10, 2019

This book was occasioned by the exhibition *Sonya Clark: Monumental Cloth* at The Fabric Workshop and Museum (March 29, 2019–August 4, 2019) curated by Susan Lubowsky Talbott, Executive Director.

Exhibition itinerary:
H&R Block Artspace at Kansas City Art Institute, MO
January 31– March 21, 2020

deCordova Sculpture Park and Museum, Lincoln, MA
October 9, 2020–March 7, 2021

Published in 2020 by The Fabric Workshop and Museum in association with MW Editions

Support for *Sonya Clark: Monumental Cloth* is provided by the Coby Foundation, Ltd.; The Andy Warhol Foundation for the Visual Arts; the Joy of Giving Something, Inc.; the National Endowment for the Arts; Maja Paumgarten and John Parker; Katie Adams Schaeffer and Tony Schaeffer; and Henry S. McNeil.

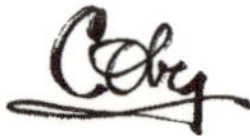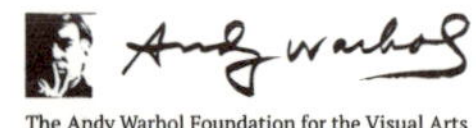

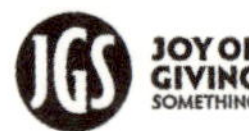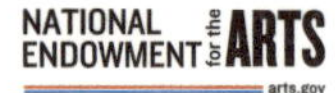

Major support of FWM is provided by the Marion Boulton "Kippy" Stroud Foundation. FWM receives state art funding support through a grant from the Pennsylvania Council on the Arts, a state agency funded by the Commonwealth of Pennsylvania, and from the National Endowment for the Arts, a federal agency. Additional support is provided by The Philadelphia Cultural Fund, Agnes Gund, and the Board of Directors and Members of The Fabric Workshop and Museum.

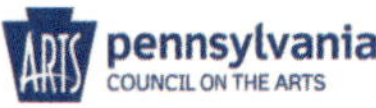

The Fabric Workshop and Museum
1214 Arch Street, Philadelphia, PA 19107
www.fabricworkshopandmuseum.org
info@fabricworkshopandmuseum.org

MW Editions
127 W 26th Street, Room 900
New York, NY, 10001
www.mweditions.com
info@mweditions.com

Art Direction and Design: Takaaki Matsumoto, Matsumoto Incorporated, New York
Design Assistant: Robin Brunelle, Matsumoto Incorporated, New York
Editor: Amy Wilkins, Matsumoto Incorporated, New York
Project Coordination: Stephanie Alison Greene and Karen Patterson, The Fabric Workshop and Museum, Philadelphia

Printed and bound at Industria Grafica SIZ, Verona, Italy

Library of Congress Control Number: 2019956548
ISBN: 978-0-9987018-6-8

Distributed by D.A.P./Distributed Art Publishers, Inc.
75 Broad Street, Suite 630
New York, NY 10004
www.artbook.com
enadel@dapinc.com

Works created through the Artist-in-Residence program were made in collaboration with The Fabric Workshop and Museum, Philadelphia.

Cover, p. 20: Sonya Clark, *Many* (detail), 2019. One hundred hand-woven linen cloths and madder dye. 18 ½ x 36 inches (47 x 91.4 cm) each. In collaboration with The Fabric Workshop and Museum, Philadephia
Pages 4, 6–7, 9: Sonya Clark works in progress at The Fabric Workshop and Museum, Philadephia
Page 10: Sonya Clark, *Reversals* (detail), 2019. Reproduction of Ella Watson's dress from the photograph *American Gothic, Washington, D.C.* by Gordon Parks (1942), dust from Independence Hall and Declaration House, bucket, water, stenciled text, and towel commercially printed with the Confederate Battle Flag. In collaboration with The Fabric Workshop and Museum, Philadelphia

Photograph Credits
Carlos Avendaño: Cover, 4, 6–7, 9–10, 20, 28, 30–33, 36–48, 50–51, 54–55, 58 bottom, 59–60, 62–69, 72–73, 84, 86–87, 90–91. Jessica Kourkounis: 34–35, 52–53, 56–57, 58 top, 70, 74–83